NAAFI, NIJMEGEN & THE PATH TO NORWAY

1st Edition

Published in 2015 by

Woodfield Publishing Ltd
Bognor Regis PO21 5EL England
www.woodfieldpublishing.co.uk

ISBN 1-84683-170-9

Printed and bound in England

Typesetting & page design: Nic Pastorius
Cover design: Klaus Schaffer

Source document
Naafi Nijmegen Norway - Blackburn [final]

Naafi, Nijmegen
& the Path to Norway

*Further adventures of a WRAF
Airwoman – 1971 and beyond*

Norra

JOAN BLACKBURN
(NEE RATCLIFF)

Joan Blackburn

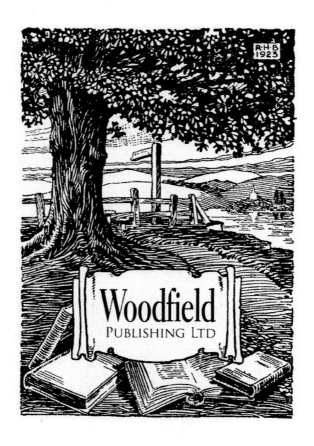

Woodfield Publishing Ltd

Bognor Regis ~ West Sussex ~ England ~ PO21 5EL
tel 01243 821234 ~ e/m info@woodfieldpublishing.co.uk

Interesting and informative books on a variety of subjects

For full details of all our published titles, visit our website at
www.woodfieldpublishing.co.uk

Dedicated to those I met
the second time around

Contents

Also by Joan Blackburn

Naafi, Knickers & Nijmegen
Adventures of a WRAF Airwoman 1959-63

It is 1959 and a teenage junior clerk joins the WRAF following a bet with her Father. What follows is a journey from the innocence of the austere fifties to the birth of the colourful sixties.

Beginning with the first tottering steps on a parade ground through to the adventure of going abroad and taking part in the 100-mile Nijmegen March three years later, it is a snapshot of the time.

Originally written in 1964, it is honest, accurate and not distorted by the passing of the years, but enhanced with the advantage of hindsight.

It shows ~ as only something written at the time can show ~ how gradually things changed, both in the WRAF and in civilian life, during that special, innocent time just before the sixties came of age.

Both informative and, at times, hilarious, it is a must for anyone who 'was there', whether they were in the services or not. At the same time, it offers a peep into 'another world' for anyone too young to have been there.

Granddad's Rainbow
Adventures of a War Baby 1939 – 1951

It is 1944 and three-year-old Joannie listens to the tall stories told by her Granddad as he tries to bring normality to a very abnormal time. Born into an upstairs/downstairs world that is fast becoming history, her grandfather, the Head Gardener at Coxhill Manor, near Chobham in Surrey, had seen it all before in 'the first lot'. Now his son, serving in the RAF in France and Malta, is just a face in a photograph to little Joannie, who one day will follow in her father's footsteps and join the Royal Air Force.

Joan Blackburn has returned, in this, her second book, to her rural working-class roots. With access to her father's RAF Record of Service and an Aunt who lived to be over 100 years old, together with the aid of her own memories, she has been able to piece together the events contained in the book accurately and informatively to create a create a realistic and warm-hearted portrayal of the life of an ordinary English family caught up in the extraordinary events of World War II and its aftermath.

The Tailor's Daughter
Adventures of Charlotte Adshead 1858 – 1929

This is the true story of the author's great-grandmother. Born in the 1850s in Clapham, London, she emigrated on her own to New Zealand at a time when to do such a thing was fraught with danger. It is also the story of Frederick Gosley, the seafarer whose life changed when he met Charlotte. It changed even more when he went blind and it took all the will-power and tenacity the plucky Cockney girl had been born with to overcome the difficulties that were to follow.

The book follows the couple through the years of their lives, which included events ranging from the sinking of the Titanic, the devastating First World War and Votes for Women until their deaths in 1929, within a few months of each other. From Charlotte's father Thomas to her Granddaughter, Lily Dorothy, it traces over a century of history.

The conversations are of necessity imagined but the facts and most of the people (including the passengers on the SS *British King*, on which Charlotte sailed to New Zealand) are real. Only a few minor fictional characters were added for the purposes of continuity.

All three books published by Woodfield @ £9.95
www.woodfieldpublishing.co.uk
www.amazon.co.uk/shops/woodfield

CHAPTER I

Back again (1971)

T he young flying officer peered at me across the table in the RAF recruiting office. He was probably about twenty-five but looked about fourteen to me. Suddenly I felt somewhat older than my thirty years. Well, at least, I wasn't quite thirty yet. If I was being pedantic about it I was one month short of this milestone in my life.

He was staring at me as if I was some sort of alien being from outer space.

"So, you really want to come back into the WRAF as a new entrant?" he smirked.

"Yes really!" I replied, at the same time wondering what on earth I was doing there.

It was 1971 - twelve years after I had joined up for the first time at the age of eighteen. Then it had been all new and exciting and against the background of being a teenager with the rise of rock and roll and the innocence of the fifties. Of course, I never should have left in 1963 when my four years were completed. I should have signed on then, but no, I came out and became a civilian. The miracle was not that I had come back but more, how long it had taken me! I had certainly taken my time.

I sat patiently waiting while the officer shuffled some papers around and looked embarrassed.

When I had joined up the first time there had been a girl in our flight who was 'ancient' at the age of twenty-five and we all affectionately called her 'grannie' so I could understand that I did seem a bit old in the tooth to be coming back.

"You do realise that you will be a *new* entrant and not a re-entrant?" he reminded me. "It will be totally back to basics – right back to basic training and learning how to march."

I was struggling now with how surreal it all was. For the past seven years I had been running a Girls Venture Corps cadet unit in my spare time and had done nothing else but teach them to march – in fact we had won prizes at figure marching competitions and drill without words of command. I probably could teach *him* how to march!

"I think I'll cope Sir," I grinned.

"Well, I have to admit we do need older airwomen in the WRAF Admin trade," he replied. He glanced at my application form again.

"I see you have been taking your cadets to do the Nijmegen Marches." He grimaced. "I did it last year – never again."

"I've done it seven times now," I informed him, "I first did it with the WRAF in 1962."

He looked suitably impressed and so he should be.

"Which reminds me," I went on, "that's one of the things I must request – if I come back in now, the Nijmegen Marches will fall during my basic training and I have promised to take the cadets again – I will have to have leave."

"You can't have leave during basic training, you must know that."

I put my handbag over my shoulder and went to get up out of the chair.

"In that case we can forget it," I replied. "I made them a promise."

The sergeant, who had been looking across the room from the safety of his own desk, spluttered into his tea in his amusement.

"I don't think me going to Nijmegen for a week will have any effect on my square bashing," I replied patiently. "I have been teaching it all this time to my cadets."

"But rules is rules. In any case, you won't be square bashing by then, you will be trade training."

The sergeant got up from his desk, came over and picked up my papers.

"It is unheard of," he grinned, "but I'll make some phone calls and see what can be done – especially for you, Ratty!"

I'd already had a vague feeling that I had seen him somewhere before and now I knew where. He caught my gaze and grinned.

"Mac!"

"Rheindahlen!" he cried. "You were in my Section – Command Accounts."

"Corporal MacCarthy!"

He pointed to the three stripes on his arm.

"Excuse me!" he replied. "Get it right, these were hard come by!"

"Well, fancy seeing you again!" I answered, completely ignoring the poor young officer who was looking on in awe. "The last time I saw you it was in Command Accounts as you and John saw me off."

"You'll see a lot of the old ones if you come back in to the RAF," he laughed. "It's a much smaller air force now."

It was a worrying thought, as there were a few that I would rather not see again – Flight Sergeant bloody Payne for one. She had been the WRAF Admin Corporal when I had first joined up and seemed to have haunted me from then on, turning up as a Sergeant in Rheindahlen in Germany and then, still haunting me, as a Flight Sergeant when I took the cadets to Nijmegen in Holland. She was there with the WRAF. The last I heard of her she was at Kinloss up in Scotland, so I really hoped I could avoid going there.

"Anyway, I think you are mad coming back," said Mac – "it's 'days to do' for me!"

"Well, that's a nice advert for the Recruiting Centre!"

"Incidentally," he said, with a beaming smile, "can you remember what John Davis's last words to you were as you left?"

I could indeed.

"He said I'd be back," I replied. "I bet he didn't think it would take this long though!"

"It's a good job we didn't have money on it!" laughed Mac.

"There is something else I have to ask," I ventured, amazed at my own cheek.

"There's more?" Both men were totally unprepared for what was coming next.

"I want to keep my old service number."

"Ah – that may be a bit tricky – you are a *new...*" said the young officer. I really got the impression that he did not get somebody like me every day in his office.

"Yes, I know Sir, I'm a new entrant – you said, but I was very attached to my number and I want it back."

"Your number will be gone in the mists of time at the RAF Record Office" said Mac politely. "You have been out far too long."

"Only eight years!"

"Only!" "What was your number Joan?"

"It was a 2832 number," I said.

"Do you know what the numbers are now? They begin with 8!"

"All the more reason why I want my number back – it was part of me and I want it back."

"I'll see what I can do – I have friends in Record Office."

He disappeared through the door and left me with the officer just as a very young airwoman came in with a cup of tea for us both. She couldn't have been more than about eighteen and suddenly I felt very envious and very old and for the millionth time I wondered if I was doing the right thing. I looked across at her.

"Make the most of it," I said, "it doesn't half go quick!"

Any doubts I had were not helped by the next bit of conversation with the young officer.

"I see you were a shorthand typist the last time you were in, but now you are coming back as WRAF Admin."

"Yes Sir, I figured that at my age I would stand a better chance of promotion once I had passed the Admin Course."

"You know what the Admin Course entails, I presume?" he went on, looking at my ample figure.

"I think so" I replied "admin and welfare of the airwomen and discipline."

I thought I knew it all, but clearly I didn't.

"You know you have to do the Physical Training Course for two weeks?" he informed me. "It's a new idea – WRAF Admin have to include it as part of their course, and the PTI's have to do a fortnight on the WRAF Admin course."

I nearly choked on my tea.

"What!!" I was aghast. "But I don't do physical training!"

"Sorry Miss Ratcliff". He was really struggling with trying not to laugh now and the airwoman sitting at her desk in the corner had given up completely. Clearly this sort of interview did not happen often. He leaned over and lowered his voice.

"I think you would get away with it" he whispered "you'll walk the Admin course and as long as you get eighty percent on that, then, even if you only got five percent on the PTI course you will get the grades needed."

I was not convinced.

"Why is it like that now?" I asked him.

"It's so that, if a PTI goes sick on a small station the WRAF Admin corporal can stand in for her and vice versa – all to do with cost cutting."

"Well, let's hope I never get posted to a small station," I replied, as Mac came back with a broad grin on his face. "I am to physical training what custard is to chips."

"Has he just given you the news about the physical training course?" said Mac. He knew that I was never the sporty type at Rheindahlen. Yes, I did the 100 mile Nijmegen March, but that was different. Any other form of sport, from athletics to netball, were very carefully avoided by me. I wasn't built for sport, never liked sport and the very idea of me taking airwomen for sport was ludicrous to say the least. I was ready to give up the whole project there and then and go back to my job as a secretary in Civvy Street until Mac spoke again.

"I've got some good news though," he smiled. "They are going to dig your number up at RAF Record Office but you will have to have a letter S in front of it, to indicate that it is a 'new' number."

Clearly the wheels were in motion.

"What about my leave during basic training?" I replied.

The young airwoman opposite listened to the conversation in awe. It was surreal.

"Can't do anything about that from here, I'm afraid," said Mac, "you will have to get special permission from whoever is in charge of you at your trade training station but I think you will be OK – the RAF are pretty supportive to cadet units these days."

I knew he was right, of course. I could never have taken the girls to Nijmegen year after year without the support of the RAF and the ATC. I thought it was worth chancing it.

Mac glanced up at the clock and I followed his gaze. It was five o'clock and the end of the day for those in the Recruiting Centre. He pushed my application form towards me.

"Are you going to sign it?" he said, and then leaned over to put his jacket on and his peaked RAF hat on his head. "It's decision time."

"It's the PTI course that is putting me off," I replied.

"It's only a fortnight," said the officer. "You'll be OK!"

I knew they really did want older women in WRAF Admin and I figured that I was in with half a chance of getting through the course. For the second time in my WRAF career I signed the application form.

◆ ◆ ◆

I sat on the packed rush hour train from Waterloo and watched the scenery whizzing by whilst deep in my own thoughts. With a bit of luck I would be back in the WRAF before I was thirty. I hadn't found a bloke the first time, and I had always vowed that if I hadn't by the time I was thirty I would make a career out of the air force. At least it would put a roof over my head and a pension in my pocket, but thirty was the deadline. Where had the time gone? Where was that young girl of eighteen whose only care was how to afford the latest record by Frankie Vaughan or knowing the words to the latest Elvis song. A child of the forties, a teenager of the fifties and a young adult in the delightful sixties, I was only just beginning to realise what a lovely era I had just passed through and I was not at all sure about the forthcoming seventies!

I felt in my handbag and I could feel the texture of a pair of knickers that had been in the bottom of the bag for the past few weeks. They weren't ordinary knickers though. They were 'passion killers', special 'passion killers' that I had received through the post from my friend Pat Seymour. I wasn't going to bring them out of my bag for the other passengers to see but I grinned to myself... *these bloomin' knickers*!

They had been WRAF issue when I had first joined up, but not for long. They eventually became obsolete and we used them for everything other than what they were originally meant for. They were long air force blue drawers that reached to the knees and were designed to cover the gap left between the top of a stocking and conventional knickers. But with the invention of tights they became rapidly a thing of the past. They instead became used as dusters, doorstops and even to polish shoes, but some were kept spic and span for hoisting up flag poles when the authorities were not looking.

This pair had begun their travelling life when I had planted them on Pat on the day we left the WRAF, although just before we parted company she had managed to surreptitiously get them back into my pocket without me knowing. Since then they had gone backwards and forwards through the post between Surrey, where I lived and Sussex, where she lived, like me, with her parents. Then, when she had heard that I planned to go back, they arrived in the post yet again, with a little note attached.

'You are stark raving bloody bonkers, but hoist 'em high!'

I decided I would have to find them a suitable resting place when I went back to Spitalgate. However, a lot of water would have to pass under the bridge before I got that far. First I had to go back to Recruit Training, then at least six months as an airwoman on an RAF station before finally going on the Admin Course and the dreaded two week PTI course. But that was a long way off. As someone once said 'I could think about that tomorrow'!

Not for the first time I wondered where the time had gone since I had originally packed the passion killers into my kit bag on my last day at Rheindahlen in the spring of 1963.

◆ ◆ ◆

~ CHAPTER II ~

"You'll be back..." (1963)

My kit bag seemed to have a life of its own as I tried to pack all my mementos of Germany into every nook and cranny.

"You are surely not bothering to take those home?" cried Liz from the corner of the room, as she watched me struggle with trying to find a space for the shoes I had worn on the Nijmegen March.

I looked at them ruefully. They were supposed to be black 'beetle-crushers' but they were grey and battered and had a huge piece cut out of the toe.

"Of course I am – I'm attached to these shoes."

"They look as though they are ready for the dustbin," joined in Kay from the other corner of the room.

There had originally been four of us in this room but Lyn had already left one month before. Now the two of them would be on their own until someone else was posted in. It just did not seem possible that now it was my turn. All I had to do was visit my office to say goodbye and then I would be on my way back to a civilian life and back to my family. Where had the time gone? When I first arrived in Germany it seemed like the next two years would be interminable – now it seemed to have gone in a flash.

I had been so lucky too. I was sure I had been on the two best stations in the RAF and they could not have been more different from each other. From trade training, where I had been taught shorthand and typing, I had been posted to RAF Medmenham – surely what must have been the smallest station ever. 'God's

Little Acre' everybody called it. We were in our late teens and it had been a whole new world of doing a job of work by day and partying in the evening. I had even joined the Signals Command Band and learned to play the cornet – not very well – and we had gone hunting for the notorious 'Grey Lady' – the ghost that was supposed to haunt the camp on the 16th of every month. We ran the gauntlet of WRAF Admin, whose sole job was to get us in at night and look after us as our parents would have wished.

Then I had come here to Rheindahlen – the biggest non-operational station in the world with a Headquarters Building that was second only in size to the Pentagon in America. Here I had grown up a bit, reaching the age of twenty-one unscathed and yet very innocent compared with later generations. It had been an adventure to go abroad and to be able to go over the border into Holland and shop in the big stores. The Dutch people loved the English and we were always looked after wherever we went, whilst back at camp we got to mix with Army and RAF, Germans, Dutch, Canadians and many more. Us girls were outnumbered by more than 100 to 1.

It became inevitable that I would be talked into doing the Nijmegen March – the 100 mile event that took place every year in Holland. Pat thought I was stark raving bloody bonkers – she always did, but it was an experience that I would keep for ever, along with the shoes.

There had only been five of us girls in 1962 that were daft enough to do it but, against everyone's advice we teamed up with the men and marched as a mixed team culminating in the famous last five miles when we all marched in triumph behind the Central Band. It was probably then that my doubts about leaving at the end of the four years began to set in. There was a feeling of belonging, of pride in ourselves and of being British.

I felt my eyes well up as I shoved my shoes further into my kit bag.

"You soft bugger Ratcliff!" said Kay, "you are going to miss us aren't you?"

I had soul searched for months, just as Lyn had done before me.

"It's no good Ratty!" Lyn had said "why put off the inevitable – we will have to be demobbed sometime."

It was true. We reasoned that if we wanted to make a career in Civvy Street we had better get on with it, although we knew, that as shorthand typists we would not have much difficulty in securing a job. Indeed, Lyn had already written to us and told us that she had secured a good job with the Foreign Office. Besides, I missed my family. My brothers, aged twelve and sixteen, were growing into young men without me even noticing. I had only been home once in the past year and maybe the grass really *was* greener on the other side and I didn't know it.

I was still slightly peeved that I had not found myself a marriageable boyfriend in all the time I had been at Rheindahlen. After all, there were enough of them. For some reason I had always fancied the unobtainable. In Trade Training at Hereford on the typing course it had been Tommy. Tucker everybody called him. However, it was not to be. He was a National Serviceman who simply did not want to be in the RAF at any price and completely bitter that he had been called up just a year before conscription in the U.K. was abolished.

"I was born one year too early hen!" he would complain.

Born and bred in Glasgow, he always called me 'hen', but his one passion had not been me – it had been his bass guitar. He was convinced that he was destined for great things in the world of Jazz. He kept in touch with me for some while but eventually the letters dried up, and I was soon to find out why when I realised he had achieved his dream. He had secured a position with Acker Bilk and his Paramount Jazz Band and the next time I saw him he was on 'Top of the Pops'.

Then, at Rheindahlen, there was Richie, who I had adored from afar. Tall, dark and handsome, also Scots and with a wicked sense of humour, he was the epitome of everything I looked for in a bloke and also called me 'hen'. There was one drawback though – one very important drawback, as it happened. He was married. So that was that.

"I know one thing," I said, as Kay and Liz got themselves ready for work. "If I haven't found myself a husband by the time I am thirty, I will certainly be back."

"It will be too bloody late then," giggled Liz as she pulled her beret onto her head. "You'll be too old – they will be calling you granny!"

"Well, at least I wouldn't have to go back to Wilmslow," I retorted.

RAF Wilmslow was where we had done our basic training and we had lived in wooden huts with twenty-eight of us to a room. The only thing holding Wilmslow together was the 'death watch beetle holding hands' had been the 'joke' that greeted everybody on arrival there. Now the WRAF were trained at RAF Spitalgate in Lincolnshire and there were no wooden huts there – just purpose built blocks with far fewer to a room. Things had moved on in four years.

Liz threw her bag over her arm and came over to give me a hug. She had to go – it was a very long walk to The Big House were she worked, and where, until today, I had worked too.

"Good luck!"

"Good luck Liz, and take care."

She had been one of the few people who I had known at Medmenham as well as Germany. Another was Jan. I was sorry not to be able to say goodbye to Jan. She was on leave and I knew was trying to get back before I left. We had been in the same room together at God's Little Acre and she was posted here some time after me. She wasn't in my room anymore but we had been friends, it seemed, for ever.

Kay was ready to follow Liz off to work. She didn't have quite so far to walk though as she was employed as a Dental Nurse in

Sick Quarters, which was not too far away at all. She gave me a hug and we wished each other well.

"Take care Kay," I smiled through my tears. "I'll write, I promise."

Then I was left alone to finish packing and get ready for my final walk to The Big House. My flight was from Dusseldorf Airport that afternoon.

Any ideas of going straight to the Big House were very soon thwarted by a group of airwoman who worked in the Communications Centre and who were not on duty until later.

"Come on," said Olive, a slim dark-haired girl from Scotland, "you have to have a last drink in the Queensway Club."

She was accompanied by Margaret and Ronnie and a couple of others who I didn't know. I suddenly felt quite jealous that they were staying and I was going.

I had been at Rheindahlen a little longer than most of them and was still getting used to calling the NAAFI 'The Queensway Club'. In the past year the centre of our universe had received a 'makeover' and now it was 'posh' with a Cocktail Bar and a very special dance floor that was the pride of 'the powers that be'. So much so that us girls had to wear little plastic caps on the heels of our stilettos to protect it from the inevitable damage that they would cause. I always thought it had been daft to choose such a soft wood, but I was just a mere mortal, and, apart from that it really was a very good makeover. There had even been a 'grand opening' attended by none other than Ronnie Carroll and Susan Maugham.

I followed the little gang dutifully into the Queensway Club and had a coffee with them.

"I wish it was me getting posted back!" said Margaret wistfully.

"I don't," cried Olive. "I have had a ball here."

Seeing her without Jan was a bit like seeing Laurel without Hardy, or Morecambe without Wise.

"I hope I get to see Jan before I go," I said.

"I'm sure she'll do her best," replied Olive.

"Remember when you both came to the NAAFI Fancy Dress dance as 'Saturday Night and Sunday Morning'?" I reminded her.

"How can I ever forget?" she laughed. "Poor Jan was mortified."

Jan had drawn the short straw and got lumbered with being Sunday Morning. Olive got to wear the tarty clothes and heavy make-up and Jan came to the dance in her dressing gown and with her hair in rollers and wearing a face pack. I did not think anything like this would happen at home – not in 1963.

All the girls were in their civvies but would soon be going back to the Block to get changed for work. I bid them all goodbye and started my walk up to The Big House.

Rheindahlen did not get its reputation for being the biggest non-operational station in the world for nothing. It was some walk across the golf course to the big Headquarters building used by the Army and NATO as well as the RAF.

As well as the Queensway Club there was another NAAFI for the Army, two cinemas, a theatre, three churches, a shopping centre, YWCA and YMCA, Malcolm Club and Salvation Army and a huge sports field and swimming pool. The list was endless and I had spent the first couple of months of my time in Germany in total awe of the place. Then there was a long period of taking it all for granted. Now, just as I was about to leave, I was back to the feeling of awe again.

The place wasn't perfect – the food was terrible, but with a restaurant in the NAAFI and our Salvation Army Café, we certainly did not go hungry. You could have fitted little Medmenham onto the golf course I was walking across and still would have space left over.

For the last time I showed my pass at the door and then walked the endless corridors to Command Accounts, where John Davis and Mac and Paddy were waiting to say goodbye.

"You'll be back," said John, as he gave me a hug.

"No, I don't think so," I replied, "we all have to adjust eventually."

Me at the sign leading into the camp, 1963.

I never dreamed that in nearly ten years' time I would bump into Mac again.

My lovely Groupy, who I had done shorthand for during the past two years, emerged from his office and wished me well.

"What about me?" he laughed "I've been in the RAF 22 years – how will I adjust?"

No, it wouldn't be easy.

Of course, there was a serious side. After all we were in the middle of the Cold War with the Russians and the Cuban Crisis. The people who worked in communications, like Jan and Olive, were always going off on exercise and being on constant alert, but most of the time it went over the heads of us 'pen-pushers' as they called us, though we each had our part to play.

It was time to go. They had been a smashing bunch to work for, especially John, who had so nagged me to do the Nijmegen March. It had given me an experience I would never forget.

"You'll be back," he repeated. "You have to get the crown to your medal don't forget."

The crown was given when you had done the march in a second year and it fitted neatly in the top of the medal, hanging from its green and gold ribbon. After that, you got a number to fit in the ribbon until it got to five and then you got a special silver medal, and so it went on. The chances of me getting the crown now were very unlikely!

They watched me as I walked down the corridor for the last time and gave them a final wave. It was now back to the WRAF Block to meet up with Pat Seymour and get the coach that would eventually take me back to Blighty. It didn't look as though I would be seeing Jan.

On my way back I passed the girls who I had seen earlier in the Queensway Club, now, all 'booted and spurred' in their uniforms and on their way to work. No doubt we were each wishing that we were in the other one's shoes. They had been joined by a few of the other girls, who, although all shift workers, I knew because of my connection with Jan.

"Give Jan my love," I shouted to Olive.

"Wish it was us going home!" she called back, as they disappeared towards the Big House and the gap between us grew wider.

"Liar!" I called, to the retreating backs.

Olive had a very nice boyfriend called Barry – she didn't want to go anywhere, except up the aisle maybe, and as she had said to me earlier in the NAAFI, she was having a ball!

I walked on across the golf course and eventually back past the parade ground and round to the three WRAF Blocks. The bus was already there and it was just a matter of getting my luggage and getting on my way. I passed Pat on the stairs of the block whilst Sergeant bloody Payne hovered in the background to make sure that we really did get on our way. Her one purpose in life had been to spoil our fun, and our one purpose had been to make sure she didn't. I think we won. I thought of all the times we had 'escaped' through the washing room window after bed check time and giggled to myself. We were never caught although we had some very narrow escapes!

There was one particular time when Lyn and I had climbed out of the window and had run through the dark woods to Radio Receivers, situated a mile away, where her boyfriend, Johnny, was on night duty, along with Richie, who I adored from afar. The only trouble was that they could spend very little time with us because they really were there to work. They even got a visit from the Duty Officer and Lyn and I were forced to dash and hide behind the teleprinter machines until the boys had got rid of him. We both crouched down silently, trying our best not to laugh, and thought he would never go.

Then there was the long walk back through the woods again and the climb into the block without waking anybody. In the end it had all turned out to be a very fruitless exercise.

Sometimes there had been much more innocent expeditions, such as getting out of the window after the block had been locked, pinching a bike and riding to a little German restaurant that was open all hours simply to get chicken and chips or for no other reason than to get 'one over' on Sergeant bloody Payne!

Pat and I gave a last look at the WRAF Block as the bus started to pull away and, together, we gave a V sign to the retreating back of our delightful Sergeant. There went one person who I hoped I would never see again. To have her on two postings was enough for anybody.

The size of Rheindahlen had never ceased to amaze me, and it seemed like ages before we had finally left the confines of the place and were out on the open road on our way to the airport. Suddenly, the past four years seemed to have contracted into nothing. In 1959 when I had signed on the time had stretched ahead like an eternity, but now it had passed, gone, and little did we realise it on that day in 1963 but we had been lucky enough to live through the most wonderful period ever. Both in the WRAF and in Civvy Street we had witnessed the 'black and white' austerity of the early fifties gradually turn into the colourful rock and roll era of the later part of that decade and the start of the sixties. We had seen Elvis in his heyday and the birth of The Beatles. It had been an age of innocence, where there were boundaries. The fact that we spent every opportunity trying to outwit our superiors was immaterial – the boundaries were there so we felt safe and secure even though we never would admit it.

We were going down the autobahn and I spotted the road sign pointing towards Nijmegen in Holland. The highlight to the whole of my time in Germany had been the Nijmegen March. One hundred miles in four days and John was right – I would have liked my crown to my medal. I had felt so proud to be in the WRAF on that day. If anybody had told me then that one day, four decades from now, the WRAF would be disbanded and, male or female, they would all be just RAF I would, to use Pat's well used expression, have said they were 'stark raving bloody bonkers!

I was brought back to the present day by the bus pulling into the airport and then all the fuss and chaos as luggage was shifted and we made our way to the departure area. Then I spotted Jan. She was waving frantically as she was being pushed through arrivals along with a crowd of families returning from leave. We waved like raving dervishes to each other and made signs in the air saying 'write soon'.

"I'll write!" I shouted, though she could not hear me, and then she was gone.

Jan had another six months to do, but I knew we would keep in touch.

Within half an hour we were in an RAF Viscount bound for the UK and within a day I had said goodbye to Pat only to find the passion killers she had planted in my pocket as her farewell gesture. Then I got the train home.

Two people who were not best pleased that I was home as a permanent fixture were my brothers. They had become used to the youngest, Richard, having my bedroom all the time I was away. True, they had to share the same room when I came home on leave but that was a small price to pay for the rest of the time when I was not there.

They had grown so much while I had been in Germany. Michael, the oldest, was quite a young man now and had already left school, whilst Richard had just started at the senior school that his brother had just left.

"Oh lord," said Mick, as he caught sight of the big bunch of 45 rpm records I was unpacking. "Now we will be subjected to Frankie Vaughan morning, noon and night again!"

"Elvis too," I replied, and Cliff Richard."

It was a time of adjustment for them as well as for me.

The only person who really understood how I felt was my Dad. He had been in the RAF twice, though it has to be said that the second time was not quite in his scheme of things. He had joined as a young man of eighteen in 1929 when the junior service was in its infancy. Then in 1938 he had come out on completion of the nine years he had signed on for, only to be recalled one year later, and one week before his wedding day, when Britain went to war with Germany. When the war ended he had a wife and a baby he had hardly seen in the intervening years, but he still anguished, just as I did, over whether he should sign on or not. Even now, he never missed a Royal Tournament or the British Legion Festival of Remembrance, and you could actually see his back visibly straighten when the stirring Royal Air Force March was played.

He glanced at some of the leaflets I had been given, along with my wages, when I left and held one of them out to me.

"You'll have to join this lot!" he said "The RAF Association – they will keep you in touch with all that is going on."

He was right of course – he was always right. I could find out where my local branch was and probably go and join in with their activities. Little did I know it at the time, but that leaflet was the first step in the long journey back. In the meantime, roast lamb for Sunday dinner and cherry pie was the most important thing on my immediate agenda.

◆◆◆

One of the first people I visited when I was demobbed was my beloved Granddad. He lived with his daughter, my Auntie Rosa, just forty minutes away at Chobham. I could have gone on the train but I was quite happy to go in the car with Mum and Dad. I adored him. Mum and I had lived with him and my Grandma through the war years and up until 1946. As a toddler I had been his shadow as I followed him around the gardens where he worked. He had been the Head Gardener for the grandparents of the singer Peter Gabriel. By now though Grannie had died and, at eighty years old, he had long since retired. He was of the 'old school' and thought it bad enough when I joined up but when I actually volunteered to go to Germany he believed the world had gone mad.

"What do you want to go to that heathen country for?" he had cried as he thumped the table. "Damn Germans!" Of course he had been involved in the carnage in the First World War and had worried when his son had been involved in World War Two. But he never stayed mad for long and he and I had a lovely mutual understanding of each other. He still had the picture of the rainbow that I had painted for him as a child propped behind the clock.

"That's Noah's rainbow!" he would tell me "sent from God to tell everyone that everything would be all right in the end."

Actually I think that, deep down, he had been quite proud of me being in the WRAF, especially when he found out that I had been to Nijmegen and had seen all the places that were so associated with the Arnhem landings and the defence of Holland.

Auntie Rosa had never married and was nearer to sixty than she wanted to be. Her goal in life was to look after the old man and to be a stalwart member of the W.I.

We sat and talked to them for some time and then Rosa produced some tea and cakes. It was good to see them, but I did have to find myself some work.

There was one thing about coming out of the WRAF in 1963. There was no difficulty in getting a job and one of the biggest employers in the area was BAC, who until quite recently had been known as Vickers. Fleets of double decker buses left Walton to take people on the short journey to Weybridge and it was also only one stop on the train.

I had no need to rifle through newspapers or go to the unemployment office. I simply walked into Reception and asked if they needed a shorthand typist.

The young girl looked in the book she had in front of her.

"What is your shorthand speed?" she said.

"100 words per minute – I have my Record of WRAF Service here."

I started to rifle about in my handbag.

"Oh, ex service – you'll have no trouble," she smiled "I think I have a vacancy that will do you if you would like to have an interview with the boss."

She picked up the phone and in no time a man in his forties, dressed very smartly in a grey suit and snazzy shirt and tie was at the desk. He had dark receding hair and was quite good looking in an older, distinguished sort of way.

"This is Mr Morrison-Davis," she informed me.

He held out his hand.

"Pleased to meet you – I'm head of the Sales Engineering Department, for my sins, maybe we can go and have a chat..."

I followed him across to another building and down a number of long corridors. It was reminiscent of The Big House, though nowhere near as big. Finally we came to a corridor with doors on either side, each marked with a person's name and 'Sales Engineering'. He pointed to a large room at the end where about thirty men were all seated at desks, scribbling away or on the telephone.

"That's the rest of the hobble-de-hoy," he said.

I followed him into the office and he sat down and gestured to the chair in front of his desk.

"Take a seat."

"Don't you want to give me a shorthand test?" I asked him, as I handed him my RAF Record of Service.

"No, I trust that little book," he said, pointing at the blue card in my hand. "If that says you were trained in the Air Force, then that will do for me."

He studied my details and then showed me into the office next door where another girl was already typing away rapidly.

"That will be your office," he gestured. "You will mainly work for me, but there are also about thirty sales engineers in there," he pointed to the main office. "You'll find their demands are very erratic – sometimes they will run you off your feet and other times there will be very little to do. Susan here is also a typist for some of them."

Within half an hour I had settled down and had already taken my first bit of dictation.

Susan was a nice enough girl and a bit younger than me. She was full of questions about the WRAF.

"How lucky are you to have gone abroad!" she sighed. "It's alright for this jammy lot." She waved her arm in the direction of the Sales Engineering office. "They go abroad all the time on business – mostly to Saudi Arabia or America."

I was sure she would get her wish before long. Package holidays were just starting to really become popular – if you had the money – and with the help of firms like BAC who churned out aeroplanes like sweeties and sold them all over the world, it wouldn't be long before the world would 'shrink' beyond anybody's wildest dreams. She was a pretty girl with a mop of wavy dark brown hair and a figure I would have killed for. Needless to say, she had all the sales engineers eating out of her hand.

BAC was a sort of tenuous link with the air force. Steeped in history, it was originally the home of Brooklands Motor Racing in 1907, then in 1914 as Vickers Armstrong, commenced aircraft production and, of course was at its height during WW2 with the Wellington Bomber. It was only comparatively recently, in 1960, that Vickers amalgamated with English Electric, Huntings and British Aeroplane Company to become British Aircraft Corporation.

The main projects that were underway as I joined the company were the BAC 1-11 and TSR2. Moreover, I was to discover that most of the blokes in the office had been in the services in one form or another, even Mr Morrison-Davis, who had been in the Navy. After all, National Service had only finished a couple of years ago.

John Morrison-Davis was also very proud of the fact that BAC still housed the offices of Sir Barnes Wallis, who invented the bouncing bomb used by the Dambusters in the Second World War. I had seen the original film with Richard Todd, so I was more than happy to be taken to view the place and to see all his drawings both of that, and of other projects he had been working on. He was nearly eighty now and long since retired but I understood that he still came in occasionally and had a potter around. This Weybridge factory was certainly a place steeped in history.

The boss had certainly been right about the erratic nature of the work. One minute we were rushed off our feet, having to meet deadlines and expected to work all sorts of silly hours to get brochures typed on time, or there was nothing to do for days while we waited for the sales engineers to produce their written work. Then, they wanted it 'yesterday'. Sue had a notice above her desk saying 'impossibilities done immediately but miracles will take a little longer'.

"This is so boring!" exclaimed Sue, as she tidied her desk for the umpteenth time during a slack period. "You see, they will be all wanting their work at once in a minute."

During the quiet times in the office I found myself thinking about my four years in the WRAF and, once more, I wondered why I had ever come out.

"Supposing I forget it all one day," I moaned. "I can remember it as clear as anything now, but I might not one day, and I don't want to forget it.

"Well, now is your chance, silly!" replied Sue. "There is nothing else to do – there's the paper and there's a perfectly good typewriter – get on with it and write a book." Funnily enough, my Dad had recently said the same thing. "Write it down" he said, "so that you never forget."

They were both right. It would never be published – I wasn't an author – but I was quite good at English and stringing a sentence together. I could write it all down for myself so that when I was fifty, or even sixty, I could read all about the things that I might otherwise have forgotten.

I put my first bit of foolscap paper in the machine and started typing, beginning with my first day at RAF Wilmslow in 1959...

"The sun glinted on scores of windows along the sides of brown wooden huts, standing in rows, like long straight worms along the side of the parade ground..."

The words flowed as I typed page after page, even surprising myself at how much I remembered.

"Goodness me," cried Sue, "that machine will catch fire in a minute!"

By the time a harassed Mr Morrison-Davis arrived with some BAC work for me to do, I had typed three chapters. I didn't hide it from him and he was most encouraging.

"If you want to do it after work," he said one day, "fill your boots – the place is open and so long as you are not claiming for overtime, I can see no harm in it."

I got on with the work I was paid to do, but I took him up on his offer and often stayed late after everyone had gone home, rattling away on the typewriter. I had bought, and learned to ride, a Lambretta scooter, so I could go home whenever I wanted, provided I did not mind my dinner being a bit dried out in the oven.

"This book had better be good," said my mother. "It is costing me in electric trying to keep your dinner warm."

Sometimes, by the time I got home both my brothers had been in and gone out again to meet their girlfriends.

Within a couple of months my book was completed and one of the older sales engineers, whose name was Frank Wilson, even got it bound for me in an A4 folder. I felt quite proud of the finished article.

"There you are, you'll be glad you did that one day," he beamed. "I wish I had kept a record of when I was in the Marines – it seems just like a dream now."

At first I decided to call it 'Another World' but Frank wasn't very impressed.

"Nah," he muttered, "much too ordinary, try and think of something that service people would understand and recognise."

I took my handiwork home with me. I wasn't very sure how my parents would react but they both read it and enjoyed it.

"You will be glad of that when you are an old lady," said my Dad proudly. However, once it had been read I buried it in my dressing table drawer along with my underwear and the pair of passion killers that had been planted on me by Pat Seymour (I made a mental note that I would have to post them back to her sometime!). It was decades before it saw the light of day again and then I remembered Frank's words about having a title that would appeal to service people. 'Another World' became 'Naafi, Knickers & Nijmegen'. However, in some ways the original title would have been just as appropriate because we were approaching decades in which the WRAF and the world in general would change almost beyond recognition to the one I was living in now in 1963. The 'beginning of the end' of our age of innocence was to happen that very year in the United States of America.

◆ ◆ ◆

I had been a civilian for six months when, quite suddenly, on 22nd November, the simple joys of the rock and roll years were shattered by events in Dallas, Texas. Life would never be the same again. It was late afternoon and I was in the big office handing in some work to John Lumsden, one of the senior sales engineers who happened to be on the phone to our office in New York. Suddenly his eyes widened and he dropped his pen on the table in front of him.

"What!" he cried. "Shit!"

Bit by bit everyone went silent as we listened to his end of the conversation.

"Oh I don't believe it – it can't be – maybe they missed!"

He put his hand over the mouthpiece and his face almost went ashen.

"They are saying that President Kennedy has been shot."

It was unreal. It had not been on our News yet or in the press. How could it? There was no instant television in 1963. Everyone sat still like statues as John listened to what was going on the other end.

"They have had it come over on the radio. They think he is dead!"

Very little work was done for the rest of the afternoon as the news came through bit by bit over the telephone from New York. He had been shot by some lone gunman hiding upstairs in a Book Depositary. He had been riding with his wife in an open topped car in the Presidential cavalcade.

John put the phone down. There was no more news. The President had been rushed to hospital and the New York office promised to phone if there was anything more to tell. Nobody really believed that he was actually dead – he couldn't be. He was an icon of the western world, the epitome of the late fifties and early sixties and the 'feel good factor'. He had charm and was good looking with a lovely young family. It was as if something dirty had been put into our lovely golden era. It was as if the innocence of the time was over and we had all been raped.

An hour later the phone on John's desk rang again and the worst was confirmed. He had been all but dead on arrival at the hospital. Many of the men had tears in their eyes as it dawned on us all that the unthinkable had happened. It was way past going home time but people still hung around and talked in little huddles.

Bit by bit the news travelled around the factory. Mr Knight, one of the directors from the upstairs 'posh' offices managed to acquire a transistor radio and finally it was official as the news was announced by the BBC and all programmes were halted as they too tried to piece together the information coming across the wire from America.

By the time we got home, images were appearing on our black and white television screens, still pictures at first, but eventually we got film of the terrible moment when the bullets struck.

The 1950's effectively did not start until 1953, when the Coronation turned a 'black and white' Britain into colour and people began to get televisions. Then the rock and roll era with Elvis and Bill Haley burst on to the cinema screens and over the radio. Our dark sombre clothes were replaced by the frothy petticoats and wide skirts nipped in with the white plastic belts and our winkle-picker shoes. There were juke boxes and coffee shops and young people still 'courted' until marriage and the word 'gay' still meant happy. But if the fifties started in 1953 the decade ended that day in November 1963. Even the Beatles started to change from the innocent young mop heads they once were. They did away with their smart suits and grew their hair just that bit longer and their music reflected the changes that were happening. They went to America and suddenly Elvis was taking a back seat as the teenagers found something different from those of us that were slightly older and remained ever faithful to our hero. Our fluffy skirts gave way to the sack dress and with the 'pill' becoming more freely available the innocent fifties were over. The nail had been finally put into the coffin of a lovely era and it was the era in which I had been in the WRAF. Even now I still had the faint inkling to go back. The world was changing but maybe the RAF wasn't, was it?

◆ ◆ ◆

It was already 1964 before I finally got around to joining the RAF Association. My social life was non-existent and I still missed the comradeship that I had enjoyed. Most of the members were a lot older than me but at least it was somewhere to go once a month and we all had the RAF in common. That was where it ended though. Darts and Bingo were not really what I was looking for at twenty-three years old. I was still in touch with Lyn, Jan and Pat and we all still marvelled at the fact that we managed to be on a RAF station where the men outnumbered the girls at something like one hundred to one and yet we failed to find ourselves marriageable blokes. It had to be something of a record! Meanwhile, my old school friends had met and married whilst I had been jiving the night away in the NAAFI and now they all had young children and lives of their own. I felt very much 'out on a limb.'

Pat was courting though and Jan had got herself a job away from home near Manchester. Lyn, or Mal as she was known at home, had settled down, for the time being at least, back with her family in Birmingham. She had been christened Marilyn and had started life in the WRAF as 'Mal' but over the years that had metamorphosed to Lyn to all of us.

Then, something happened at one of the RAF Association meetings that would change my life for the next eight years and yet, perversely, put me on the road towards rejoining the WRAF. We were visited by two ladies who were officers in the Girls Venture Corps. They were looking for someone young enough to run a Unit which they hoped to open up in the old buildings at Brooklands, already occupied by the ATC, and yet old enough to 'take charge'. It was like an omen and ideal for me since I already worked there.

In the interim, much to the amusement of both my brothers, I was getting about on my scooter so I had the wheels to come and go as I wished and I could also go and see Granddad without relying on Dad all the time.

"Good lord, keep death of the roads!" laughed my brother Michael when he saw me spluttering to a halt in front of the house on the Lambretta.

"She is going to be a mod," giggled Richard.

"You see," I retorted, "this will be ideal for me and maybe I can start getting a social life."

"Not running a GVC Unit you won't," said Mick, whose life revolved around the Scouts.

I ignored their taunts and soon I had driven over to Brooklands to see the ATC Unit there and find out more about what was involved. The ATC Officer was a nice chap, tall and dark, and he seemed to be in total control of about thirty boys, who were all busying themselves with various activities around the old building at the side of the old race track which had seen better days but once had countless cars speeding around it in the 1930s. Now it was just a curved slope with weeds showing through the cracks.

Although the building was ancient it was pretty solid and the inside was ideal for the cadets, with two good classrooms and a drill hall. Even more importantly, it had a kitchen. Upstairs there was an office, which would be for the ATC when they were there and for me when my girls were there.

"We are off to Nijmegen this year," said Flight Lieutenant Evans, "maybe if we have the girls here they can come with us as well next year!"

The crown to my Nijmegen Medal suddenly seemed a real possibility and I needed no more persuasion. Within a matter of weeks I had a uniform, the unit was advertised in the paper, I had adult helpers, and I had over thirty young girls between the ages of fourteen and sixteen who all wanted to be GVC cadets and be like the ATC. Any notion I had to return to the WRAF was suddenly put on the back burner.

At first the ATC Officers came along to help us and give us tips, and then we had a visit from the Senior Commandant from the Area and I was armed with all the advice I needed. I passed all the appropriate tests and received my warrant card to become a Unit Commandant and I was back in WRAF uniform again – this time with three rings around my arm like a senior officer. The whole family thought that this was totally hilarious.

"Well, that's one way of getting a commission," laughed my Dad. The rings were a different colour to those worn by a 'real' officer and I did have a different cap badge, but it still caused much amusement in the household every time I got dressed up and went tootling off on my scooter. Pat Seymour thought I was 'bonkers' and told me so often enough in her letters – so much so that she got the passion killers back in the next post!

In the meantime things were really beginning to move with the formation of the new Unit. We even had our own Unit Flag, which we made ourselves. Well, at least I designed it and the Vicar, the Reverend Herbert Jones, found somebody locally to make it. My Dad made the pole it hung on from an old broomstick that he sanded down and varnished. It was all truly a joint effort and it was hard to believe that two short years ago I had left the WRAF for good, never to be seen again. Or so I thought. Now, if we ever did get to go to Nijmegen we would have our very own flag to take with us.

The idea of me rejoining the WRAF just seemed further and further away.

FLAG FOR VENTURE CORPS

A flag for Brooklands Squadron of the Girls Venture Corps is to be presented to the committee tonight (Friday).

The flag, which is the corps' first, was made by Miss Gladys Frith, of Sunny Barn, Lower Pyrford Road, Pyrford. It was designed by the Commandant, Mrs. Joan Ratcliffe, and bears the crest of the G.V.C. organisation.

The Rector of Byfleet, the Rev. Herbert Jones, who is also Chaplain to the Squadron, will make the presentation.

The flag will go abroad with the squadron to Holland in July, when members are to again take part in the annual walk from Nijmegen.

The Rev. Herbert Jones, Chaplain in the district Girls Venture Corps, holds the new flag.

Joan Blackburn / Naafi, Nijmegen & the Path to Norway ~ 31

~ CHAPTER III ~

Retracing Old Steps (1965)

I did the second Nijmegen March of my life in 1965 but this time it was very different. This time it was 75 miles, as all my cadets were under sixteen. I took some holiday from my job at BAC and, with the help of the ATC, we arranged for the cadets to take part. This time, though, it was a long journey by coach and boat and suddenly I felt very 'old' with all the young fourteen to sixteen year olds. I was all of twenty-four!

It was the first time that GVC cadets had taken part in Nijmegen and we would not be there at all if it wasn't for the help of the boys. For me it was great because, just for once, I was in charge. It was me that took them out practicing and me that decided what uniform they would wear. I remembered all too vividly us WRAF struggling around the course in the pouring rain on the third day of the march and how the wet turned the hems of our skirts into whips that thrashed against the backs of our legs, so much so that in the end we all rolled our skirts up around our waists and turned them into minis. I had taken special note of the sensible Israelis in their lightweight skirts that ended just above the knee and decided that I wanted something similar for the cadets. I had another lady helping me with the girls. She was tall and slim, dark haired and wore glasses and she was a bit older than me, being well into her thirties. Her name was Pauline Harris and between us we worked out what we would do.

"How about denim?" said Pauline, "Maybe we could get somebody to make them?"

I wanted our uniform to complement the ATC uniform and not be too far removed from the WRAF.

"Perhaps if we wore the WRAF summer blouses!" I volunteered, "I'll get in touch with Headquarters and see if they can get us some."

"And the GVC hat," said Pauline, "they must have the GVC hat and the Union Jack on the sleeves of their blouses."

We were really getting quite enthusiastic about the whole project.

In the end it was my mother that got the job of making all the skirts in a lightweight blue denim and we made sure that they all finished above the knee. The finishing touch, because they were young and I wanted another distinguishing feature were long white socks. After making fourteen skirts, including mine, Mum got to the point where she never wanted to see another denim skirt again!

"The things I do for you and to keep the peace!" she said one day, as she completed yet another plain blue skirt and ironed it ready for its prospective owner. "My life was so much easier when you were away in the WRAF." She didn't really mean it and I know, for a fact, that she had missed me. I think though that, even she was beginning to hope that I would be married by now and that she might have grandchildren on the way.

In the meantime we did our practicing every weekend around the local streets and soon I was retracing my steps to Nijmegen. Something I never dreamed I would do again.

It was lovely though to see the old place again and to see the familiar Nijmegen Bridge as we approached the town in our coach. There were the usual smiling happy faces and the festoons of orange and green flags all over the place.

"Isn't it great!" cried Fay who was one of my older cadets at sixteen, "I can't wait to get started."

They had all had plenty of practice and so I was fairly confident that they would do well, and furthermore I would get the crown to my existing medal.

Me with the cadets.

It was a glorious day as the coach dropped us off at the school where the girls would be staying. The boys were being taken on to the men's camp at Heumensord. Even in 1965 we were all kept well separated and I knew it would be the same for the WRAF, who were bound to be there as well. Indeed, as we walked up the steps we bumped straight into two of them. One of them I recognised straight away. I could not believe what I was seeing. It was only Sergeant bloody Payne, except that she was a Flight Sergeant now. I could not miss the crown above her three stripes. She looked as surprised as me, especially when she saw my uniform with the three rings around the sleeve.

"Oh my God, it is SACW Ratcliff with her rings up!" she sneered, and then burst into peels of laughter.

"Hello Flight!" I sneered back, actually quite surprised that she remembered me. I looked down at the rings on my sleeve. "Bet you never thought you would see them on me!" I laughed.

Then just to make matters even funnier, one of the younger airwomen appeared from one of the rooms in the school and saluted me. I kept a straight face and saluted back.

I could see she was just about to make a retort at the girl but, just then, one of the WRAF Officers appeared and she swallowed her words. I thought she was going to explode! Of course I was not a proper commissioned officer but we all gave each other the courtesy and the young officer treated me as one of her own. I mentally put 'two fingers up' to Payne and continued on to our classroom which, as always, for the purposes of the march, became our billet.

I learned later that Payne was still the SNCO at Rheindahlen and I sent up a silent prayer of thankfulness that, at the end of the March, I would be going home to my job at British Aircraft Corporation and not back with her. Being a civilian did have its compensations!

After a few hours it felt as though I had never been away and the cadets were certainly the centre of attraction with everyone, including the older WRAF girls, who thought the denim skirts and white socks were a brilliant idea. I got a few caustic comments from Payne because we were only doing seventy-five miles, but nothing I couldn't cope with. Bloody woman.

At least I wasn't on my own with the cadets. Pauline Harris had come with us and there was also a WRAF Officer who kept a friendly eye on us. I also had one brave cadet to act as our cycle orderly.

For the second time in my life I was able to see the wonders of the Tattoo that marked the start of the march and took place in the Stadium each year and once again I experienced that thrill as the Central Band of the Royal Air Force took its place in the arena to the sound of the RAF March Past. Even now, my blood still turned 'air force blue' at the sound of it. The cadets

Nijmegen Bridge.

sat in the stands and watched it all in awe just as I had done two years earlier. Once again we were treated the skirl of the Pipes from the Laarbruch Pipe Band, the various Army Bands and the German Army Band and countless others. Then there was the sight of the children running onto the Arena carrying their flowers and the continuous cheering of the friendly Dutch people and the participants alike. I had seen it all before but it still came up fresh. But this time there was one thing different. This time I was responsible for these young girls, who were little more than children. This time I had to make sure they got their beauty sleep ready for the March the following day. They didn't need much persuading – by the time the coach arrived back at the school all the girls were ready for their beds and despite their excitement they all slept soundly and were up with the lark for the first day of the Nijmegen March.

"Come on, rise and shine!" It was Pauline's voice that woke me from my slumbers but I wouldn't have slept much longer anyway. Already there was a cacophony of noise as the cadets fell over each other in their efforts to get ready. I could also hear the sound of other women running up and down the corridor outside in a bid to get to the toilets and get themselves sorted out for the forthcoming day. I looked at my watch.

"Five-thirty!" I gasped "Oh my gawd, what am I doing here?"

Nothing had changed. It was still bread with 'hundreds and thousands' on top, just as it had been two years earlier, for breakfast. This was washed down by a cup of cold tea with no milk and sugar. The Dutch certainly knew how to live it up!

The girls were so excited though and were soon ready. I already felt so proud of them in their skirts made by my mother and their long white socks. They looked fresh and smart and everyone complimented them on their turnout.

We were soon making our way down to the Market Square where the marching started from and we strolled along in groups, some of them walking along talking to the WRAF girls. All my girls called me 'Ma'am' which greatly amused Flight Sergeant Payne.

"Oh look at everyone all lining up Ma'am," cried an excited fourteen-year-old called Jenny. "Do you think we will complete it all right?"

"Of course you will," retorted Payne, "how can you lose with Wing Commander Ratcliff in charge."

I ignored her and we made our way to where the ATC cadets were also lining up getting ready to start. Little did I know it then but it was the start of another five Nijmegen Marches that I would do with the cadets. If anybody had told me then that this would be the case I would have used Pat Seymour's words and said they were 'stark staring bloody bonkers'!

I heard myself saying "By the left – quick march" and we were on our way, on the first day of the 1965 Nijmegen Marches and even this early in the morning the crowds were out on the streets to encourage us on our way. This time though we had to follow the blue arrows which denoted the route for those doing the 75 miles.

It wasn't long before the cadets were the 'sweethearts' of the march. Very early on in our marching practice we had learnt that it was much more fun if we did arm exercises as we marched, clapping our hands above our heads and then in front of us and behind our backs in sequence. All of this as we sang our favourite marching songs. Pretty soon we had made a name for ourselves and people were looking out for us.

For most of the day we followed the same route as everybody else, following the arrows which were on wooden boards at each turn in the road or at each crossroads. Eventually though, our blue arrow pointed in a different direction to the green arrow of the one hundred mile marchers and we found ourselves with a short cut, which knocked approximately six miles off our route. Then we were marching through the country lanes with all the other younger groups such as the ATC and the Army Cadets and the Scouts and Guides and also different Dutch civilian groups. All the while the girls did their arm exercises and soon we were back with the main crowd and entering the Rest Point. We seemed a very long way from my job at British Aircraft Corporation but deep down I knew that this was just the start. There would be many more years of bringing the cadets back to Holland. How this would pan out with the continued niggling feeling of wishing I was back in the WRAF I did not know. I couldn't do both! Then, I heard the sound of Flight Sergeant Payne's voice as she shepherded her team into the Rest Point and they all flopped down on the grass. Quite suddenly, the pendulum slipped back in favour of Civvy Street!

◆ ◆ ◆

All the cadets completed all four days of the March and received their medals and huge bunches of flowers and they too had experienced the delight of doing the last five miles behind the

The last five miles.

Central Band. All the RAF Groups had waited for each other at the last Rest Point – RAF, WRAF, ATC and GVC and we had all marched in together, doing a smart 'eyes right' as we passed the saluting dais, and the Commander-in-Chief of RAF Germany rose out of his chair and took the salute. There was not a dry eye among the cadets and I guessed I might have unwittingly provided a few new recruits for the WRAF when they were old enough to join.

I had some very tired but very happy young girls to take home on the Saturday following the march. I bid farewell to the friends I had made among the WRAF.

"Make the most of it," I told them. "It goes far too quick!"

"Back to the day job now, Ratcliff?" The dulcet tones of Flight Sergeant Payne never let me down.

"Yes," I replied. "You won't have to call me Ma'am anymore!"

There were peels of laughter all round. She was sporting a very heavily bandaged foot and had all but limped in the last five miles.

She caught my gaze. "This is what happens to those of us that do the full march," she grinned, "not half a march, like some people I know." I refrained from pointing out that I had done the full march some two years earlier and that we had completed it in a mixed team with the men, something that was unheard of in those days. But I couldn't be bothered.

Now it was back to the real world and my job with BAC and I still had a future to plan. Yes, I had a future to plan but I never would forget the past and I continued to keep in touch with all my friends, Pat Seymour, June and Jan and, of course Lyn.

◆ ◆ ◆

CHAPTER IV

Back to Square one (1971)

Was it really six years ago since I had taken the cadets to Nijmegen for the first time? Now here I was, back in the WRAF for real. What WAS I doing to myself? I was nearly thirty and I had to start all over again. This time though I would be doing my Recruit Training at RAF Spitalgate. I thought fondly of Wilmslow, which is where I had done my training the first time, but time waits for no man and the WRAF had moved on. Now they were in Blocks instead of billets.

I had travelled up on the train with a group of young girls and I already felt ancient. I felt even more ancient when I saw the WRAF Admin Corporal who would be in charge of us. I was shepherded into one of the Blocks along with twenty or so ladies, none of whom were above eighteen and immediately I was told I was to be in charge of them all and given a white band to wear on my arm.

"I wonder what we have all let ourselves in for?" muttered a young Scottish girl who had plonked herself down on the next bed to me. Only the surroundings had changed. The people and the comments were just the same as they were in 1963.

"I wish I was starting again at the age of eighteen," I said wistfully.

"Quiet everyone!" The Corporal was just about to make herself heard.

"I am Corporal Jones and will be in charge of you for the duration of your stay at RAF Spitalgate," she announced. Then she looked in my direction.

"I understand that you have been in the WRAF before Ratcliff?" She looked down at her notes. "I see you have kept your old number. We won't be able to say 'get your number dry' to you will we?" she chuckled.

I chuckled back and wondered for the umpteenth time what I was doing here. I had a good job in Civvy Street and I was doing well with the cadets. Now I had handed over my GVC to somebody else and already, I had heard, some of them had left, and there was talk of them amalgamating with the ATC. In some ways I felt as though I had let them down, and for what? I looked around at the rest of my flight. Some had gone to other rooms in the Block but there were ten girls in this room. They all seemed very nice. I wondered how I would get on learning drill from scratch when I had never left it. It all seemed very surreal.

Eventually the Corporal left and suddenly I found myself surrounded by everyone wanting to pump me for all the information they could.

"Why did you come out?"

"What have you come back in for?"

"Where were you stationed?"

"Hold on!" I laughed. "I can't answer you all at once – what I can advise you though is to get yourself unpacked and get your bed spaces ready and then you will have more time in the NAAFI later, that's if Corporal Jones lets you out."

I found myself thinking of Pat Seymour and chuckled to myself. She really would think I was 'stark raving bonkers' now.

Meanwhile I had kept in touch with Jan and June over the years and also with Lyn. Jan and June had been with me when I had been stationed at Medmenham and also at Rheindahlen, although June had been married by then. Lyn had been with me at Rheindahlen and, at one point had shared a flat with me during my intervening years in Civvy Street. I unpacked my case and lay on the bed while the younger ones chatted among themselves. I found my mind drifting back to the Heath Bridge Club flat and Lyn.

◆ ◆ ◆

1967

The cadet unit went from strength to strength and I took them back to Nijmegen again. I also continued with my journeys on my scooter to British Aircraft Corporation. By now Sue had left and I was the Secretary for most of the Sales Engineers and also for the Chief Sales Engineer. At home my parents and my brothers were long suffering as usual. They put up with me coming and going on the scooter and Mum occasionally had the job of making yet another blue denim skirt for a cadet. My brothers, who were fast becoming young men, were starting out on their working lives and manfully putting up with me continually playing records of Frankie Vaughan and Elvis Presley and sharing a room. At the same time though, I had the feeling that I should be standing on my own two feet. Up in Birmingham my friend Lyn felt the same. She had just acquired herself a job down in London and was looking for somewhere to stay. At first she found a flat near to where she worked but it was lonely. Like me, she missed the WRAF but had soldiered on in Civvy Street working for the Foreign Office. I scoured the papers for a suitable flat. At least I knew my brothers would be happy if I left home. Richard could at last have my room to himself.

My mother wasn't so sure. "People will think you are not happy at home." she said. "Whatever will the neighbours say?"

"Mum, I am twenty-six!" I retorted. "You don't want me here any more than I want to be living with my parents."

"It's about time you found yourself a bloke!" said Richard. "It's time we got you married off."

"Who'd have her?" laughed Michael, as he dodged the book I threw at him. I loved them both really!

I soon found a flat right by Weybridge Station called the Heath Bridge Club. As the name suggested it was a Bridge Club but there were also a number of flats in the place. They were all pretty pokey but if it gave me my independence then I was happy. I drove up on my Lambretta scooter and had a look at the place. It consisted of one main living room, two bedrooms and a kitchen. My mother came to see it and wasn't all that impressed but agreed that it was very convenient being so near to where I worked and to where I ran the Cadet unit.

"It will save on petrol Mum," I insisted.

"Oh well, if you must you must!" she said "but you come back home any time you want to, you understand?"

Assuring her that I certainly would, I roped in my long suffering father to help me remove my possessions into the flat and within a few days I was joined by Lyn.

She hadn't changed much from when we had shared a room back at Rheindahlen. She had courted a chap called John all the time we were there but it never came to anything. Once Lyn was demobbed they went their separate ways.

"I don't know," she said to me one day when we were bored out of our skulls in our tiny living room, "here we are, twenty-six and still we haven't found ourselves a man. What the devil is the matter with us?"

"They don't know what they are missing," I replied.

I think though it was then that I started to think that maybe, just maybe, it might not be too late for me to return to the WRAF, not necessarily for a man, but for a long term career. I made a mental note that I would give myself until I was thirty.

We were at the flat for a year and then, after much soul searching, Lyn decided to give up her job and go back to her family in Birmingham. I was not at all happy because I was forced to move into a much cheaper bed-sit within the same building. My mother was even more disgusted and thought I had gone completely mad.

They thought I had gone even madder when I changed my job and joined a Temping Agency! BAC was becoming a shadow of the company that I had joined in 1963.

The rot had started to set in when the Wilson Government cancelled the TSR2 aeroplane project. Everyone had been devastated and there had been so many redundancies. It was the first time I had seen grown men weep and John Morrison-Davis was one of them.

"You wait and see," he moaned, "there won't be an aircraft industry in this country in ten years' time." Little did he know how near to the truth he was. Even the mighty Concorde was in danger of being scrapped.

I decided it was time to move on. I had my scooter and I could go anywhere. Who knows – maybe this was an omen and my new life would begin now.

"Look at this!" remarked my Dad one day as he scoured the local paper. "Look, an Isetta car for £40. Do you know you can drive one of these with a motorbike licence?" They were words he would come to regret but would cause a considerable amount of laughter in the forthcoming years.

I had been at home for the weekend. I was still very partial to my mother's Sunday Dinner and it was pouring with rain.

"There you are! That will keep you dry!" said my Mum.

I had a bit of savings and I figured that I would get about £30 for my scooter so suddenly it seemed a very feasible prospect. After all, it wouldn't be hard to drive if I already had a licence for it. I had mastered the scooter OK. It was being sold by someone not too far away.

"Let's phone them up!" I cried. "You never know, they might keep it for me until I sell the scooter." We hadn't long had the phone put in and I think, right now, Mum was beginning to regret that too!

"For goodness sake girl, it's a Sunday afternoon!" My Dad shouted as I rushed to dial the number in the paper. He was too late. The chap on the other end of the phone answered and he agreed to keep it for me until we could go and have a look at it. Within days I was a 'car owner', if you could call my little maroon bubble a car. It slowed down when I tried to take it uphill and

A bubble-car similar to mine.

RAF Spitalgate.

I had been known to be overtaken by milk floats. As for the engine, my mother could hear me coming down the road long before I came into sight.

◆ ◆ ◆

"Stand by your beds!" I was aroused from my thoughts and the picture in my mind of my little red car changed to the gates of Spitalgate as those all too familiar words, that I had not heard since 1959, rang round the room. I didn't quite know whether it was sheer bliss to hear them or horror! The memories of cadets and my little car evaporated through the roof as I bolted up and stood to attention. I thought yet again, *"what am I doing here?"*

Well, all this was certainly different from my Recruit Training at Wilmslow. I felt that the rest of my flight did not know they were born! They had electric floor polishers! Electric floor polishers, I could not believe it. We had old fashioned bumpers, like a brick on the end of a pole and we had long wooden billets with a stove in the middle. Now we were in purpose built blocks with central heating. They always used to say that 'the only thing holding Wilmslow together was the death watch beetle holding hands'. I looked around this smart room in the block and decided that there were unlikely to be any death watch beetle here. One thing had not changed though, and that was the cry of 'stand by your beds', and the bulling and the early mornings.

The chattering of the younger girls stopped as we were introduced to our Senior NCO in charge of us. I was in such a daze that I only had just taken on board that I was in B Flight. I had been in D flight the first time round. She looked in my direction.

"I understand that you have special permission to take leave when you first start your trade training," she said. She said it in a tone that made you think that she did not believe what she was saying.

"Yes Sergeant," I replied. "It's to take the GVC Cadets to Nijmegen, but it won't affect my Recruit Training."

Everyone looked totally shocked.

"Well, you are very honoured airwoman," she smiled. "Taking leave like that is totally unheard of."

"I'll be a Ma'am during that week" I thought to myself and found it difficult not to laugh out loud. I also slightly wondered what it had to do with her as it would not be her granting the permission. It would be the Senior NCO at the start of my Admin Course.

I soon found out that we were in Trefusis Forbes block, although all the Blocks looked alike, just like blocks of flats and very different from the wooden billets I had been used to at Wilmslow twelve years earlier. Was it really twelve years? I could scarcely believe it.

At Wilmslow it had been the strains of Cliff Richard singing 'Living Doll' that could be heard coming from the NAAFI. Now it was 'Knock three times on the ceiling' that we heard as we wandered down to the centre of our social activities for the first time. It would be a song that would haunt us for the next six weeks.

On top of everything else decimal currency had been introduced just a few weeks ago. None of us could get used to the idea, least of all me. Suddenly our wages consisted of ten pences and five pences and you couldn't say sixpence anymore, it was 2½p.

"I will never get the hang of this," said Julie, a pretty dark-haired girl from Yorkshire. "I am sure we are being conned. A shilling isn't a shilling anymore, it's five pee."

In the end I poured my purse out onto the counter.

"There you are, a cheese pastie and a coke please and take your pick."

I let the NAAFI lady rifle around and take the money she wanted. It put me in mind of arriving in Germany and being confronted with Marks and Phennigs.

"Give me good old pounds, shillings and pence any day of the week," said Vanessa, who also came from Yorkshire. "Look at this, it's like pretend money."

We were like little old ladies trying to put the world to rights and it took a few records on the Juke Box to get us jiving and forget about the money – for the time being at any rate.

We enjoyed our supper and strolled back to the Block in plenty of time for bed check. It was going to be a long six weeks for some of them.

It didn't take long for uniform to be issued and for the flight to take its first tentative steps onto the parade ground. Poor Corporal Jones, she had a motley lot to lick into shape. I couldn't help but think that my cadets would show them a thing or two when it came to marching. They were figure marching champions. Also, there is nothing more difficult than being taught drill from scratch when you actually know how to do it.

"One, pause, two," yelled our Corporal. I must have stood out like a sore thumb. In the end I found myself, at first, helping her, and within a few days she was leaving me to supervise the flight as they did the basic first steps.

What am I doing here? I thought to myself for the umpteenth time.

But the time did pass by quickly and I sailed through all the RAF History and the Drill. Not so hot on the PE but nobody minded that. It didn't seem like five minutes before we were all gathered into the classroom to be told our postings. I just hoped that the RAF were going to be kind to me.

"I bet you would like to know where you are posted to Ratcliff?" she looked straight at me. She had remembered that I was going to ask for leave the minute I got in the door of my new station.

Now she was talking. That would be interesting. I hoped it would be near enough to home to make it easy for visiting. I didn't fancy ending up in the wilds of Scotland at Kinloss or

Lossiemouth or somewhere – much as I liked the Scottish girls and still had friends among the Scots from last time.

"You are posted to RAF Northwood in Middlesex."

"Wow!" I said out loud, "well that will do for me!"

It was just a ride on the underground and then the train from Waterloo to get home, or forty minutes or so by car. At least it wasn't in the middle of nowhere. I wasn't sure that I fancied the idea of being an ACW for six months but needs must.

The Passing Out Parade didn't disappoint. Perhaps it didn't have the same freshness and wonder as my original one, but we still had the Central Band and we still had the Vulcans flying overhead. I stood to attention and when we did the 'eyes right' I could see that there was not a dry eye among the younger girls, many of whom had their parents present to see the proceedings.

I.had a bit of a feeling of de-je-vu but it didn't take away the majesty of the occasion. We took the General Salute and then, to the strains of The Dambusters March, we left the parade ground. I glanced up at the RAF Ensign on the flag pole at the edge of the square. I didn't think it would be a good idea to hoist Pat Seymour's passion killers up it this time. Not if I was going to be WRAF Admin and in charge of discipline. I had to do something with them though and it was with thoughts of this that I marched back to the Block ready to pack my bags for my trip home and then my journey to Northwood.

"B Flight – Dismiss!" That was it – for now. Those who had families present went off into little huddles and others wandered into the Block. What was in store for me? Was this really the start of the rest of my life? When had the desire to come back into the WRAF changed to the real thing?

There were lots of hugs and promises to write and see each other again but I knew I would be unlikely to see many of the airwomen. Also, as I was going in for WRAF Admin I would be back here again in six months time to do the Admin Course.

In actual fact it was a total waste of time me being there at all, other than for the purpose of being issued with my uniform.

It was the rules though. If you had been out of the WRAF for the amount of years that I had it really was back to square one, irrespective of the fact that you already knew the RAF History and the Drill and had continued it on with the GVC Cadets. That counted for nothing. I just hoped it would count for something when I came to speak to my new Senior NCO.

◆ ◆ ◆

"Northwood!" exclaimed my Dad when I got home and told him my posting. "Why that's only just up the road – not far from where I was stationed at Uxbridge."

I think Dad secretly wished it was still him. Coincidentally - he had been in the RAF twice though I didn't know that at the time. He didn't want to say too much because he didn't want to influence me. He knew it must be my decision and my decision alone. He had joined in 1928 when the RAF was in its infancy and had stayed in until 1938, only to be called up again in 1939 when the Second World War broke out. I was five when he was finally demobbed in 1946. Little did he know it then that I would be following in his footsteps – also twice!

"I can take you there," he volunteered. "It will be a nice run out for your mother and I in the car."

So it was that Richard got his room back and, after a couple of days at home and looking up my old school friend, who now had two children, I was on my way to RAF Northwood. I think Dad just wanted to be nosy and see what it looked like.

In actual fact RAF Northwood was mostly HMS *Warrior*. The Commander-in-Chief Home Fleet had moved to Northwood some years earlier and had taken most of it over. Consequently when we stopped at the Guardroom there were RAF on one side and Navy on the other. Of course Dad and Mum couldn't come any further. I kissed them goodbye and Dad helped me with my kitbag and case.

"You take care," said Mum, "and don't get up to any mischief."

"Huh!" I laughed. "Dad said that to me back in 1959 and look where it got me!"

They left in good spirits amid much laughter and I walked down the road to the WRAF Block. The WRENs Block was on the right hand side and the WRAF Block on the left right opposite the NAAFI. Well, at least that was sensible!

It was a nice WRAF Block, just two stories high and of course there was the usual notice about twenty yards before you got to the door – 'no RAF beyond this point'.

I wondered if they had forgotten about the sailors!

I walked inside and knocked on the door of WRAF Admin. I was greeted by a middle aged Warrant Officer who looked like she had been in the job for ever. She was quite plump and had greying hair and a uniform jacket full of medal ribbons.

"Welcome to Northwood!" she beamed "I'm Warrant Officer Stephens, I'm glad you can type – I shall have plenty of that for you."

I didn't mind that. As far as I was concerned I was just killing time until I could get onto the Admin Course.

My new boss had been about a bit and most of her medals were earned in the war. Now she was just killing time until her demob when she would be fifty-five. She reminded me of a female version of Group Captain Panton, who I had worked for at Medmenham all those years ago. He had been a fighter pilot

and one couldn't help feeling the aura of someone who had the air force flowing through their veins, just like my Dad.

I lost no time in asking about Nijmegen but she was ready for me.

"Already know about it," she said. "The carrier pigeons in the air force move swiftly."

"Will it be OK?" I asked.

"Well, it is unprecedented when you are so early in your Admin training," she said, but it has been agreed."

I was overjoyed and amused to see that she already had the leave pass ready for me. I would be away again within a week.

"Your room is just down there on the left," she said, "and, by the way, watch out for the squirrels!"

I hadn't a clue what she was on about but. As it happened, it was the end of the day and the daytime inhabitants of the Block were all arriving back from tea in the Mess. I found myself entering the room at the same time as my new friends. Well, at least, I hoped they would be my friends. All three of them were ten years younger than me.

"Hi!" I ventured, "nice to meet you."

I saw them glance at my sleeve, which at the moment was devoid of any badges.

"I know," I laughed "no laundry marks yet. I'm afraid I am a trainee WRAF Admin and I go straight to Corporal when I have finished my courses."

"Oh Blimey," gasped a plump flaxen haired cockney girl, whose name was Betty, "that's going to cramp our style girls!"

"I'll try not to, I promise."

They looked a bit apprehensive but they did turn out to be quite friendly. Of course it wasn't the same as June, Jan and Jessie who had shared my room on my first posting the first time round, but how could they be? It wasn't their fault that I was the grannie of the room.

Besides Betty there was an Irish girl with a mass of freckles and black hair called Maggie and a very slim, dark-haired girl called Audrey. All three worked in the Comcen.

I'd had a good feed of my Mother's cooking before I left home and she had armed me with some cake to bring to camp, so I shared some of that. I didn't really need a proper meal. Instead I spent the time getting unpacked and getting used to my surroundings. Maggie put the kettle on and made some coffee and they sat down and tucked into the cake.

"Your mother makes smashing cakes," said Audrey, as she made short work of a big slice of chocolate sponge. "This beats the Mess."

I quickly found out about the squirrels that the Warrant Officer had mentioned.

It was a boiling hot day and they had the windows tight shut. I made a move to go and open them.

"I wouldn't do that if I were you," said Betty.

"Oh no!" piped up Audrey. "Squirrels! They will have this cake in a minute. If you don't believe us, have a look..." She moved to go and open the window just enough for me to put my head out. "Only a minute though, or they will have all our cake."

I quickly put my head out of the window and I had never seen so many squirrels in all my life. It was like a swarm of them. They were everywhere, up the walls and trying to get into any window they could. I shut the window quickly.

The WRAF Block backed immediately onto a large area of oak trees and clearly the squirrels had bred and nobody had bothered. In fact they quite liked them but, although cute, they were pests.

"Oh, they will have your cake as soon as look at you," said Audrey, "they are quite tame."

"I left the window open when I went to work once," said Betty, "and when I came back they were all over the room. Even tore open the packet of powdered milk we had. Had to shoo them out, damn things."

Well the idea of being at Northwood wasn't all that exciting but at least it had something that I had never come across before at a RAF Camp. A flippin zoo!

That evening we all went over to the NAAFI. It was a very small one in comparison with some I had been in but it was cosy and it had the main things necessary for the wellbeing of any service man or woman – namely a counter that sold food, a bar, a Juke Box and a TV Room. Betty and Audrey entered into a discussion as to who was best, The Beatles or the Rolling Stones and suddenly it was as if the clock had been put back. Of course they all wanted to know about me and why on earth I had chosen to come back again.

"You must be barmy!" said Betty. "I can't wait to get out."

"Ha-ha," I laughed, "you say that now, but in ten years' time you will be saying that it was the best years of your life – trust me."

I don't think they really believed me. Eventually I left them to it and wandered back to the Block. It had been a long day and I had to be up with the lark to see what Warrant Officer Stephens had in store for me, though I wouldn't really be starting properly until Monday. It was Friday tomorrow and most people would be going home if they lived near Northwood. Normally I would have done so but it seemed a bit daft when I had only just arrived and would be leaving again next week. I resolved to spend the weekend getting to know the camp and writing letters to my friends such as Lyn, and Jan and June. Oh and of course Pat Seymour – never forget Pat Seymour. It seemed odd to be in the WRAF without her somehow but she was courting strong now and due to be married.

Within a week I was back home again. My brothers were not too happy as, once again Richard had to vacate my bedroom.

"Blimey!" said Mick, "you have only been gone five minutes!"

It was great to be home so quickly though and, after all, I only pinched my room back for a couple of days. Then I was off to meet up with the cadets again.

This time our team consisted of youngsters from other Units and so despite the amalgamation of the GVC with the ATC we had a large team of 25 girls. Fortunately though, my mother did not have to make all the skirts. They had been told what denim to buy and given the pattern and all turned up with the correct marching uniform.

Nothing had changed though. All the Nijmegen excitement was still there and we still all got the thrill when we saw Nijmegen bridge for the first time. Even Flight Sergeant bloody Payne was there with her group of airwomen. There was no getting away from her. I sent up a silent prayer, to whomsoever was listening, that I would not come across her again in my new service life. After all she was WRAF Admin and I was going to be WRAF Admin. It was feasible. God forbid. However, this time I was also an airwoman, not just any old airwoman, but the lowest of the low. An ACW. You don't get any lower than that. She knew it too. Somehow she had found out.

"Oh it's ACW Ratcliff with her rings up again!" she laughed when she saw me arrive. "Don't tell me they let you out?"

"Oh, I have my contacts Flight!" I said. "besides, I am ACW1 now!"

It was odd to think that here I was in Nijmegen while everybody else from my flight were starting their trade training.

This time I had taken a bike with me. I missed having a cycle orderly last year and I remembered how we had been so grateful for Jamie, our cycle orderly in the RAF Germany team back in 1962. He had been our rock, riding forwards to see what lay ahead and bringing back water when needed.

It was only an old bike and I intended to push it most of the way but it would be handy to use. Besides I had not had the practice this year as I'd had in the past. Well, that was an open invitation for Payne.

"Oh, got to cheat now, have we?" she crowed, "doing it the easy way – on a bike!"

In actual fact it wasn't the easy way at all. For one thing you are pushing the darn thing and for another, if you do choose to ride it then you end up riding backwards and forwards and doing twice the distance. I just ignored her. This year I would get a Cycle Orderly medal to add to my collection.

Nijmegen never changed and yet it came up like new every year. It was a remarkable thing. There was the same early morning walk down to the start, the same banter with the boys who had turned up from Heumensord and the same thrill as the Band played us out of the town and out into the open countryside, following the streams of marchers who were ahead of us and leading those that were behind, and everybody singing. Always the singing and the cadets clapping their hands in time to the beat. Nothing changed and yet all seemed fresh.

I found myself wondering if this would be my last Nijmegen. Where would I be this time next year? Goodness only knows.

I marched along at the side of the girls, pushing the bike, and watched them as they sang. Now they were young women and some were already talking about going into the WRAF themselves. There was Fay, who had been with me right from the beginning, and young Penny now doing her third Nijmegen with me. A team of Gordon Highlanders caught us up and we temporarily swapped hats with them for a while. They really looked quite silly in our grey GVC hats while the girls were swamped in their black hats with the red ribbons down the back. It wasn't for long though. Soon our pace became too short for them and so they overtook us and we waved them goodbye and found ourselves in front of a team of Swiss. There were always teams of Swiss.

Then the first Rest Point and I heard myself saying the usual phrases like, "Don't sit down for too long, keep moving or your muscles will seize up. Who wants the loo?" They all went running off in the direction of the temporary loos. In 1971 those hadn't changed either. They were still the holes dug in the ground with a tarpaulin around to preserve ones modesty.

Then we were on our way again. I cycled on to see how far the next Rest Point was and to get a chance of taking photographs of the other teams. Then I noticed the familiar sign sending the seventy-five mile teams off on their short cuts whilst the over sixteens continued on their way. I cycled back to where they were marching along behind a team of Danish.

"Not far now," I told them. I took a couple of bottles of water from out of my cycle basket and passed it round and they strode out with renewed vigour.

Now the crowds at the side of the road were getting bigger and little children ran out to hold their hands for some of the way. Somebody sprayed cologne at us and then a Band came and joined us and marched us through a village while the people cheered. Suddenly RAF Spitalgate seemed a million miles away.

Then, out of the corner of my eye, I spotted Pauline Harris. She had all but taken over the cadet unit now that I had left and she was acting as our back up. She had hitched a lift with the RAF and was waiting for us on the corner of the street and would march with us for the rest of the way just in case any of the cadets needed any attention to blisters.

There were no blisters and on we went until there, in the distance, we spotted the familiar sight of the Nijmegen Bridge. That would be the end of our march for the day. Just three more days to go.

So it went on, the partying in the town and then the second day, and the third day where the route took us past the famous Groesbeek cemetery where there were so many Canadian War dead. Here the cadets were to stop singing and we marched past in respectful silence. It was here that I did regret having a bike, because the route led us over some quite large hills. I could have well done without it. At one point Fay took it off me and pushed it for some of the way while I marched.

Then the lovely fourth day, the day of the Gladioli, when all the Dutch arm themselves with bunches of this majestic flower and then rush out to put them into our arms on the last five miles.

"Well done the young ones!" they would shout. "Well done the British!"

I had done it all before but it didn't lessen the thrill. Occasionally we passed or were passed by Payne and her WRAF team amid the usual banter.

"Come on!" they would shout, "what are you waiting for?"

"She's alright," cried Payne, "she's got a bike."

"At least you haven't got my bum," I shouted back, as they overtook us.

"I wouldn't want your bum!" she retorted.

Then we would overtake them to cries of, "Come on, keep up, we have to get back before dark!"

Finally, we turned left into the last Rest Point, where we all smartened up and lined up in formation with our 'air force blue' counterparts. The WRAF went off into their own groups and so did we as we waited for the main air force contingents, the ATC and the Officers from Cranwell. We would all march in together.

The first time I had done the march back in 1962 our team had been immediately behind the Central Band of the Royal Air Force. This time we were the juniors, the babies, and we were towards the back behind the ATC. We had our GVC Flag with its broom handle pole and I got young Fay to hold it aloft as we took up our positions. Then came the order to 'Quick March' and we all filed out of the Rest Point onto the main road into Nijmegen. The thrill was the same, the air force blue blood running through my veins was the same. The cheering was the same, the flowers and then the salute to the Commander-in-Chief. Then another corner and it was all over except for the back slapping and the laying on the floor in the dust.

Pauline Harris turned up with the envelope containing all our medals, including my cycle orderly one, and then we all hobbled back to the school whilst the boys and men boarded the bus that would take them to the tented camp. Even in 1971 we were all kept separated. The building was alive with the sound of screaming girls in all different languages. The Dutch Girls, the Norwegians, Germans and of course the WRAF, many of whom I knew by sight. I walked along the corridor and there was a long queue outside one of the classrooms for the 'blister parade'. In any language the blisters were the same, as were the screams. The Dutch idea of treatment still hadn't changed – a piercing with a sharp instrument into the blister and then iodine poured into it. I passed on that one!

When I went into the room the cadets were already getting changed into cleaner uniforms ready to go off down the town.

"Come on Ma'am," cried Fay Carter, "you have to come with us – and you Mrs Harris."

Pauline had just come in and flopped on the bed.

"We all must be mad!" she gasped. She hadn't even done the full march. She was just there for assistance.

The daft thing was that I was useless at sport. With a jolt I remembered that I still had that to come. The Physical Training side of the WRAF Admin Course! It was a laugh just thinking about it where I was concerned. Oh well, it wouldn't be over six months – maybe a miracle will happen before then and I would become a Size 8 and athletic. Instead, at this moment in time, I just had a good pair of feet and a bit of tenacity. That would have to do.

Nijmegen was in full festive mood when we finally arrived at the Square in the Centre of town. Pauline and I had given the 'hundreds and thousands on bread' a miss and we called into a café and indulged in mushroom omelette and chips. Feeling much more human, we joined the cadets under 'the yellow umbrellas' and joined in the singing and the dancing. The 'umbrellas' were bright plastic sunshades over the tables in the town square. There were bands playing on every street corner and even a barrel organ for good measure. We were joined by a group of the Gordon Highlanders who were totally fascinated at the cadets' novel uniform with the denim skirts and long white socks. However, if any of the men had designs on any of the girls they were sadly out of luck because nobody was in any fit state. All they wanted to do was sit at the tables and sing. It was the end of yet another Nijmegen and tomorrow we would be off back home and I would have to go back to Northwood and continue where I left off.

On the coach home I was almost oblivious to the singing of the cadets as my mind wandered back to a couple of years ago and how events turned out.

Nijmegen Medal and Cycle Orderly Medal.

~ CHAPTER V ~

A Blast from the Past (1968)

My whole world came crumbling down in 1968 when my beloved Granddad died. I had done many temping jobs since leaving BAC and one of these had been in the Pathology Department at St. Peter's Hospital in Chertsey. It was certainly different.

My job was to work for the Chief Pathologist and he was a nightmare. He would not allow Snopake or rubbings out on any of his letters so if you made a typing error, even if it was right at the end of a perfectly typed letter, he insisted that it be typed all over again. It certainly taught me accuracy! I also had to wear a white coat all the time and I felt like I was a 'pretend doctor' walking around the place. I didn't like it at all, but then Granddad was admitted to hospital and I postponed any ideas I might have about moving on. At least I was on the spot to go and visit him, whilst Dad and Mum could come and see him in the evenings.

I walked down the ward and saw him lying in the bed with his eyes partially closed. He looked so frail all of a sudden. This mountain of a man who had been my rock since the day I was born. I held his hand. This man who had been at Ypres in the First World War and in the Home Guard in the Second.

"Joannie!" he smiled, "so glad you came to see me." He tried to lean up on his arm but couldn't. "I hope you are going to keep away from those old Germans!" he said, perfectly seriously.

"Don't worry Granddad, I will!" I replied.

It was strange to see him lying here. He had been a gardener all his life and had started out in the Bothy at Althorp House, the home of Lady Diana's parents. Then he moved south where he met my Grannie, only to have his life turned upside down by the First World War. He never would talk about it, although I did know he had been in the thick of it.

"I remember the going," he would say, "and I remember the coming back. It's the bit in the middle I want to forget!"

I sat for a while, holding his big, brown, strong hand and remembered the times when he worked for Mr and Mrs Gabriel and I was a toddler who followed him everywhere. He allowed me to pick the strawberries and fed me grapes (or diddy-dottems as I called them) and always, always he had time for me.

I gave him a kiss and left. I walked into the car park and sat in my little red Isetta car and wept as if my heart would break. I could hear the sounds of the No.1 Record being played on a Radio somewhere. I believe it was coming from the windows of one of the offices. It was Louis Armstrong singing "What a Wonderful World". It was so appropriate. It summed the man up. The following morning Dad informed us that he had died and my world as I knew it crumbled.

Having my own flat had seemed a good idea at the time, but after Lyn left and went back to Birmingham it was never the same and I found myself spending more time at home than at the flat, which defeated the object a bit. I was also still devastated about Granddad and didn't like being on my own to mope. It just made it seem worse somehow. Being at home was only marginally better though because everyone felt the same. He had been the centre of our family.

"Why don't you leave that bloomin' old flat and come home!" said my Mother, who was always wondering what the neighbours might say. She was always convinced they would think I had fallen out with the family.

"Take no notice," piped up Michael, "you stay where you are, I like having my room to myself."

It was ridiculous, here I was, only two years off from being thirty and my social life was non existent and, much worse, my

Granddad had gone. Only my little bubble car lightened the atmosphere, as it was a continual source of amusement to everyone. It kept breaking down and it was always Mick or Dad who got the job of trying to sort out the problems that the temperamental vehicle offered to them. More often than not one or the other of them would have to come and tow me home if I broke down.

"Damn thing eats up oil," said Mick one day. "It ought to go on the dump."

"You are talking about the car I love," I replied. But I hung on to it. It was so useful to get me backwards and forwards to cadets even if it did pop and squeak and slow down when I went uphill, or milk floats overtook me. Many was the time that I had to phone up my Father to come and rescue me and I got towed back home for yet another repair job by my long suffering brother.

"Not again!" he would cry.

Then came the turning point. The point at which my desire to put the clock back and go back into the WRAF became a distinct possibility.

I had to attend a meeting up in London at GVC Headquarters with the Chief Commandant. In her capacity as the 'boss-in-chief' she had a lot of connections with the WRAF still. After the meeting I found myself in conversation with her and I told her how much I missed it.

"Why don't you go in as WRAF Admin?" she said, "they would jump at you at your age – they want the older ones and you would get your Corporal tapes after a year."

"Oh I can't," I moaned. "Everyone would call me Grannie." I remembered one of the girls in our flight at Wilmslow. She had been just twenty-three or so and we had always thought of her as an 'old woman'.

"They wouldn't call you Grannie if you were a Corporal," she smiled. "Not that I want to lose a good GVC Officer," she hastily added, "but your Unit is well established now and you have people who can take over."

That was very true. A vision of Flight Sergeant Payne went across my brain. If anyone had rapid promotion it was her. A Corporal when I had been at Wilmslow and a Flight Sergeant within about five years. It was incredible. Maybe that was my destiny – to be single and have a career in the WRAF. I was immersed in thought on my way back on the train.

I thought of all my friends who were now married with children. It just hadn't happened for me. It wasn't that I had not had the boyfriends. I had. The two most important ones had been Tommy and Richie, both Scots and both unobtainable. One married to the idea of being in Acker Bilk's Jazz Band and the other – married!

There had even been a Gordon Highlander that I had met at Nijmegen. We exchanged letters and he came to visit me at the Heath Bridge Club and met my parents. My mother was horrified. He arrived in his kilt, he smoked incessantly and she couldn't understand a word he was saying. It was something else that wasn't to be. No, it all made sense – I was destined to remain an old maid and devote my life to the air force. By the time my train arrived in at the station my mind was made up.

The next few months were taken up with handing over the cadets to others, giving in my notice and leaving my flat, and, sadly, watching my lovely little Isetta being taken to the dump.

"I think I will have to pay them to take it away!" laughed Mick, as he and Dad towed it on its last journey.

He was right, of course, and it was also my last attempt at driving a car. If I had any vehicle in the future, it would be a push bike.

Richard was just anxious to have his room back.

◆ ◆ ◆

Now here I was, already having done my Recruit Training, completed Nijmegen again and now, after saying goodbye to the cadets, I was on my way back to Northwood to continue my future in the WRAF.

I was tired, I ached all over but I was pleased to have taken the cadets for one last time and I found it hard to hold back a tear when I said my goodbyes to them when our coach arrived back at Brooklands. Who knows where I would be next year, or whether I would be able to get leave to take them. I might be on the other side of the world for all I knew. All that remained now was to get home and my Dad would give me a lift back to camp.

Mum came with us just to be nosy again and this time she actually came into the Block. Dad, of course, was not allowed anywhere near. The room was empty but, thankfully, very clean and shiny ready for inspection the following day.

"It's nice," she said, "what a nice airy room."

Her curiosity satisfied, I escorted her back out to the car, where Dad was waiting. I gave them both a hug and watched until they were out of sight. I was unlikely to be stationed this close to home again. It dawned on me that I had hardly had a chance to get to know the people in my room properly. I had been there less than a week before I had swanned off to Nijmegen. It really was unprecedented.

"Welcome back!" said Warrant Officer Stephens as I arrived at the Admin Office the following morning. To be fair, I thought it was about time she got some work out of me. I spent the day, doing some typing for her and then finding my way around the station properly and discovering where everything was. That evening it was my chance to spend time with my new room-mates, or two of them anyway. Betty, Audrey and I put on our civilian clothes and walked over to the Junior Ranks Club, though everyone still called it the NAAFI. It wasn't very far, just a few yards past the WRAF Block boundary, and it was a lovely summer evening. It was a far cry from the hustle and bustle of Spitalgate and a million miles from Rheindahlen, where it had been like a big town, housing thousands of service people. A trillion miles from Nijmegen, where I had just been, and the thousands of people from all over the world marching the 100 miles and cavorting in the evening. There were a few naval types talking in groups but otherwise the place was quiet. I could hear the sound of the television coming from the TV Room and there was the clink of glasses as the barman got ready for the evening.

"Oh blow this!" cried Audrey, "let's put something lively on the Juke Box. I let them get on with it. Time was when at the sound of the first beat I would have been up jiving but I sat and watched while they danced around to the sounds of Bobby Darin. I was beginning to recognise the airwomen and there were a few that were my age. All were friendly and we began to have a pleasant evening chatting away. They were always interested in my previous service career and whatever made me go all the way back to being an ACW again.

"Oh well, I will get my tapes by the end of the year and then I will be able to charge you all if you are naughty," I laughed.

I looked at the clock and toyed with the idea of going back to the Block for an early night when a lanky figure who was propping up the bar caught my eye. There was something about the way he stood, the black wavy hair and the way he leaned on the bar with a pint in his hand. He was in uniform and sporting some Corporal tapes on his arm. Clearly he was on duty. No, it couldn't be, I was dreaming! I could feel my jaw dropping and my blood racing. It was the subject of my affections ten years ago at Rheindahlen – he who had broken my heart, or so I thought at the time. It was Richie! He caught my gaze and our eyes met. At first he looked at me as if he couldn't believe what he was seeing, and then it clicked in his brain that it really was me. I was oblivious to the rest of the girls looking on as I tried to fathom if it was really him or just somebody that looked like him. In the films or in a romantic novel it would have read "and they saw each other across a crowded room and their eyes melted" or words to that effect. As it was we both uttered two words at the same time.

"Bloody hell!"

I didn't miss the wedding ring on his left hand as he held his beer in mid-air like a statue. He had changed in looks – so much thinner now and with grey bits in the black hair but the twinkle in the eye was the same and the grin.

"That's Richie MacDonald, do you know him?" hissed Betty in my right ear.

"A blast from the past," I hissed back, as I rose from my chair and walked towards him. One thing hadn't changed – it was me that walked towards him and not the other way round. In the world of the romantic novel this is 'where my future would be assured and we would fall into each other's arms with our unrequited love restored'. But this was the real world and already I was realising that I was not that twenty-one year old romantic anymore and actually, although I was drawn towards him, I didn't fancy him in the same way.

"How do you come to be here hen?" he said as he put his beer down and gave me a hug, much to the amusement of the younger girls in the background.

All the same, I wished that he didn't call me 'hen'. I did used to melt when he used that word.

"I've come back in," I explained, "and I am just here killing time before going on my WRAF Admin course."

He had just picked his beer up again and all but choked as he spluttered in laughter.

"What!" he laughed, "after all those times at Rheindahlen when you tried to avoid WRAF Admin and climbed in and out of the Block windows, now you want to be one?"

"Hey hey!" laughed Audrey from the table, where quite a little gang had gathered, "you never told us that Joan."

"What's with this Joan nonsense?" said Richie, "it's Ratty girls!" Slowly, all my secrets were being laid bare.

Then I had to ask the sixty-four thousand dollar question.

"Are you still married?" I whispered.

I'm not sure if I was disappointed or relieved at the reply.

"Oh yes hen, and I have a three-year-old baby boy."

"Oh!" I mumbled, feeling ever so slightly deflated.

"Come on," he said "I have half an hour before I go on duty, let's go and talk about old times." He looked across at the very interested faces at the coffee table. "In private!" he laughed.

I picked up my bag and followed him to the television room, which was now empty.

"We know where you are going!" they all sang.

I ignored them. One thing I did know about Richie, I did trust him even after all these years. The magic had gone but I couldn't forget how I used to feel either.

He had never hid from me that he was married when we had met at Rheindahlen, but his wife was in the UK and never did join him in a married quarter. He had remained on camp and lived as a single bloke. I had fallen for him hook, line and sinker, though I knew it was a relationship that wasn't going to go anywhere. We were just a bit of romantic company for each other and it never got any further than a kiss and a cuddle as we said goodnight after a few beers in the NAAFI. I would have killed for it to go further. He was just trying to 'have his cake and eat it too'. Then it was all over when he had been posted back to Scotland and I never saw or heard from him again – until now.

It was just as well that it hadn't gone any further because the more we chatted the more I realised that the magic had definitely gone. We talked for a while and he told me about his postings and where he had been in the past ten years. *"It took him a long time to get round to having a baby."* I thought. Then put the thought to the back of my mind. After all, it was his affair.

He looked at his watch. "I'm going to have to go hen!" he said. Then he said something that I totally did not expect and which really took me aback. "Would you fancy babysitting for me?"

What! I was speechless for a minute.

"It's our wedding anniversary next week and I would like to take Margaret out," he was saying. "You could come round and we could give you some tea. We would be back by midnight."

One thing about being an older airwoman, I did not have to worry about bed check. That was for the younger ones. My brain was racing. I had been much too close to this woman's husband ten years ago and I really did not want to meet his wife. I had visions of her being some gorgeous looking blonde who would leave me looking like a very poor second. At the same time I was curious and the idea of having a tea that wasn't cooked in the mess really appealed. I found myself saying 'yes' despite myself. It didn't hit me straight away but it was a reminder of the man's lack of sensitivity and cheek. Later, I realised that I had probably had a lucky escape!

"That's great!" he replied. "I've got to go now but I'll see you about and I'll pick you up from the WRAF Block after you finish work next Wednesday."

A few people had wandered into the TV room and someone was messing about with the controls to get the News. It was all about the events in Northern Ireland. I was sick of hearing about the events in Northern Ireland and the continued squabble between north and south. They were going on about throwing people into Long Kesh prison without trial. I was starting to think the world was going mad.

"Come on!" he said as we both got up, "I'll walk you to the Block."

We strolled out of the NAAFI, or Junior Ranks Club as it was now called. They would always be NAAFIs to me. It was now quite dark and a lovely starlit night. If anybody had told me ten years ago that I would be standing under the stars with Richie a decade later I would have said they were crazy. Or to use Pat Seymour's words 'stark raving bloody bonkers.'

He kissed me on the cheek and we went our separate ways. Ten years ago I wouldn't have washed. Now I walked into the Block and gave my cheek a rub. Did I dream all that?

~ CHAPTER VI ~

A Learning Curve!

My job as an ACW trainee Admin really started in earnest now. Warrant Officer Stephens informed me that I would have to take turns working in various parts of the camp to get used to all the different aspects of the WRAF. This part of the Admin Course was clearly designed for people who had never been in the services before and, like everything else thus far, it was just going through the motions for me. All the new stuff would start on the Admin Course which, as things stood at the moment, was likely to be next year. Basically I felt as though I was back on Pool Flight and that they were hard put to know what to do with me.

"Personnel Department this week," said the Warrant Officer, "you can go there in the mornings and then come and type out my Rosters and notices in the afternoons."

As she was speaking there was a timid knock on the door.

"Oh yes, I nearly forgot," she said quietly. "I've got a couple of kids to charge – you can stay and watch if you like."

"Oh my gawd!" I thought. *"I've been there and got the T Shirt."* I had also worked for eighteen months in the Personnel Department when I had been stationed at Medmenham. So far there was nothing new. I'd better get used to it.

"Come!" she shouted in her best Warrant Officer growl.

The door opened and two young girls appeared. They looked so frightened I felt sorry for them. I wasn't sure right then if I could be strict enough to be WRAF Admin. I stood to one side and tried to make myself as inconspicuous as possible. They could have been me a few years ago.

"You were caught trying to get back into the Block at one o'clock in the morning," she growled. "What do you have to say for yourselves?"

Both girls stood silent, not daring to speak and then one of them tried to scratch her arm.

"Stand to attention when I am talking to you!" the Warrant Officer shouted. "Speak! One of you speak! Baker... what have you got to say?"

Poor little LACW Baker quivered. "I'm sorry Ma'am, we went into London and missed our train back."

"You went into London and missed your train back?" The older woman mimicked. "Where do you think you are, on holiday, and that you can just come and go up to London as you please?"

"Sorry Ma'am," said the now shaking LACW Baker.

I was seeing Warrant Officer Stephens in a new light. One I had not seen before. I knew she was acting but I wondered if I could act that well. Now she turned on the other girl.

"LACW Robbins!"

"We did run for the train," she ventured, "we really thought we would get back in time Ma'am."

"Well you have to learn your lesson," She moved towards her desk and started shuffling some papers. From my vantage point I could see it was all done for effect.

"You know I could charge you for being absent without leave?" she barked. "If I put this forward to the WRAF Officer you could get seven days restrictions for this plus a blot on your records."

The girls stood to attention and seemed ready to take what was coming to them.

"As it is," said the Warrant Officer, "I am feeling in a nice mood today so I will let you off with a warning." Then her voice softened. "Go on, off you go and don't you cross my path again or it will be a charge for you."

The two girls almost cried with relief and left the room a lot more quickly than they had entered it. As soon as they were gone the Warrant Officer burst into laughter.

"There you are Ratcliff," she grinned, "that's how it is done, it's all good acting."

Well, they certainly were not acting when I had been put on jankers for 'causing a disturbance and failing to carry out an order' all those years ago at Medmenham. I got seven days!

◆ ◆ ◆

I did a couple of days in the Personnel Department typing letters for the Group Captain and in the evening we went to the NAAFI. I had to supervise the Bull Night on the Monday but that didn't take long and I was able to have another drink with Richie and confirm again that I would indeed babysit for him, though I couldn't believe I had said I would. I wrote to Lyn in Birmingham and told her of my meeting with him. She remembered him well, of course, as he had been part of our little gang. I had a letter back from her expressing her surprise but she had a surprise for me too. She was considering re-entering the WRAF as well.

"I've had enough of Civvy Street!" she wrote. "Mom's OK now and so I think I might follow in your footsteps." She always referred to her Mum as Mom. Lyn had always looked after her parent, who was on her own, but now her brother and cousins were growing up and there was much more support. She had been biding her time and simply waiting to see how I would get on. She had never met anybody after her romance with John had finished. Maybe she hoped that it wasn't too late to find somebody else. As far as we knew John was now very firmly married with a family. It seemed as though we were both 'missing the boat'.

Richie was there to pick me up at the WRAF Block at 6pm when the working day was over. This time he was in civvies and he still looked as dashing as he ever did.

"Thanks for doing this hen," he said, as if it was a normal occurrence and there was nothing incongruous about it.

"That's OK," I replied.

"By the way, you look nice," he said gallantly. "I like that dress."

I was convinced that his wife would be somebody really gorgeous and so I had made an effort and tried to make myself look a bit decent and had my hair done. I did not want to be shown up too much.

It was only a short distance to the married quarters and he opened the car door for me, led me up to his front door and turned the key. The smell of steak and kidney pudding met my nostrils. Then I met Margaret – and she was not what I had expected.

She was fat – very fat. Now, I was no lightweight and would never be a size 10 but Margaret was two of me and very short, so she was as wide as she was tall. She had dark hair and it was scraped back into a bun. To say I was shocked would be an understatement. I still wondered why she had not joined him in Rheindahlen when we were there. We were immediately joined by a bonny three-year-old.

"This is Douglas," said Richie. "Say hello to the nice lady Douglas."

"Hello." He ran off to do what little boys of three do when they have a box of toys to distribute round the room. Actually he was the image of his father with black wavy hair and a very cheeky smile.

"Hello hen!" said Margaret. "Come away in and have some tea." She was certainly nice enough. She ushered me into the living room, which was tidy enough, though I felt it was in need of decoration. But that wasn't their fault. That was the fault of the MOD. He caught my eye when I looked at the pock marked paintwork.

"I know, I have been on at them for ages to come and do it!" he said "I'll be doing it myself soon."

The steak and kidney pudding was lovely, as was the jelly and ice cream we had afterwards. Douglas sat in his high chair and did justice to his.

"Don't worry," said Margaret, "you won't have tae do anything because I will put him to bed before we go." They were only going out for a drink and frankly it was worth babysitting for my ex-boyfriend just to get the steak and kidney pudding.

Afterwards I helped Margaret to wash up while Richie got the child into his pyjamas and ready for bed.

"I'll leave the television on for you," said Richie when he came downstairs. "You won't hear anything from Douglas." It was all so surreal.

I'd brought a book with me and I settled down into the armchair while they got ready to go out. I suppose I should have been flattered that he trusted me.

"You go and have a good time," I said, when they finally came down the stairs. She had made some sort of an effort and had put some make up on. She had quite a pretty face but she was certainly not what I had expected.

"We will be back in time to take you back to camp," said Richie. Then the door slammed and they were gone.

He had been right, I did not hear a peep out of Douglas. I even had a little creep upstairs and looked in his room. He was out cold, sleeping the sleep of a very active three-year-old.

I was able to catch up on *Coronation Street*. I hadn't seen it for ages and it was nice to find out what Ivy Tilsley and Vera Duckworth were doing. There wasn't much else on and so I resorted to my book and eventually dozed off. Therefore the evening went very quick and in no time at all I heard the slamming of the car door and the key turning in the lock.

"Thank you so much!" said Margaret, "have there been any problems with Douglas?"

"Not a peep!" I replied. They clearly had a nice time and Margaret looked as though she had a few too many. She flopped down in the other armchair while I stood up and made ready to go.

"Now let me pay you," she said.

I wasn't having any of that. I felt guilty enough, without taking money off them as well.

It was still warm as I followed Richie to the car and within a few minutes he had driven back to the WRAF Block. Yet another surreal moment in this surreal return to the Air Force was over. I just hoped it would not be too long before I would get my Admin Course. He gave me a hug for old time's sake and a kiss on the cheek and then was gone.

When I arrived back into the room I was just in time to spot Audrey and Betty climbing in through the window. They stopped in their tracks when they saw me.

"Oh blimey, banged to rights!" said Betty. I was not happy.

"For goodness sake, what do you have to take a chance like that for with me sharing your room?" I snapped. "You know how it puts me on a spot – I'm supposed to report you." Of course I would not have done so, but I remembered Warrant Officer Stephens tip about the acting. Trouble was I was not a good actress and I ended up bursting into laughter. Of course there were no restrictions on what time I had to be in but they were under age. By rights they should be charged.

"Just a tip for you," I laughed, "the next time you try and creep in through the window don't have the flippin' light full on. Not least because of the squirrels. Already there were some crawling up the wall and trying to get in after our biscuits.

For me Northwood was the most boring of stations. They were in the throes of handing over to the Navy entirely that year and RAF Northwood was more HMS Warrior than anything. All the right hand side as you came in the gate was taken up with Naval offices and Communication Centre and there were WRENS in their very smart uniforms rushing about looking official. Nobody ventured into the left hand side other than a few matelots who seemed to delight in getting drunk in our

NAAFI. Usually they were helped on their way by some officious looking SPs or 'snowdrops' as they were commonly known.

I went home most weekends and most weekends my Dad would bring me back. Thus the time was ticking by until I could go on my Admin Course. I seemed to do nothing else but go and work wherever they needed a typist or I was in the Block counting sheets or checking that the washrooms and drying rooms were clean and they were not short of light bulbs. In the meantime I did meet Richie occasionally in the Junior Ranks Club but I declined any more offers to babysit, despite the temptation of his wife's cooking. I had visions of kicking my heels like this for another six months when Warrant Officer Stephens made my day.

I had just been to collect the post and was busy putting it in the airwomen's pigeon holes when she tapped me on the shoulder.

"I have news for you, madam!" she said. "Your Course has come up early!"

That did take me by surprise.

"They have brought it forward and you can go back to Spitalgate in October". She waved a copy of the Preliminary Warning Roll in front of me and there was my name – ACW Ratcliff posted to RAF Spitalgate, together with the date.

"Mind you," she went on, "it will probably turn out to be a bit longer because you will have the Christmas break in between and..." she paused for full effect "...it will be all through the winter."

Well, we were already all but through the summer and October was not all that far away. I was thrilled that I would not have to wait longer than necessary. I had seen enough of Northwood. I had left the RAF as an SACW and had come back as an ACW2. The least I wanted was to just get my Corporal's tapes on my arm whether I would be paid for it or not. I could have hugged her but refrained.

"Thanks Ma'am," I said, and carried on with my duties with a new incentive. There would be much to learn in the next few months.

◆ ◆ ◆

I think Maggie, Wendy and Betty were quite sorry to see me go. They were all twelve years younger than me but we had some laughs together, especially on the occasion when I had caught two of them coming in through the window, and they always hung onto my every word when I told them stories about the Nijmegen Marches and my time in Rheindahlen. By the time I had finished they were all hoping they would get postings to Germany. I hoped they wouldn't be disappointed because the WRAF was changing. I could see it already.

I spent almost my last night at Northwood having a drink with everyone, including Richie, and listening to the Juke Box. It seemed to be always 'Chirpy Chirpy Cheep Cheep'.

"Not like our day is it?" I looked across at Richie, "you couldn't jive to that like we used to jive." Already I was beginning to sound like an old woman.

"No hen," he laughed, "we could do with a bit of Elvis." It still sent a shiver up my spine when he called me 'hen'. It was his way of saying it.

"We could indeed." I went over to the Juke Box to see what they had and I found "Good Luck Charm".

"There you are," I said "A trip down memory lane."

"Oh, I love Elvis," cooed Betty. Everyone loved Elvis. He had gone out of fashion for a little while, especially when his Manager had contracted him to doing all those awful films. Of course he had done some lovely films, such as 'Blue Hawaii', 'Jailhouse Rock' and 'G.I. Blues', but there had been some rubbish ones as well, designed simply as a vehicle for his songs, and to get him out to the wider world. Videos had yet to be invented. Now he was making a comeback in a big way. He had lost weight and looked wonderful whether it was in his black leather all-in-one suit which he wore for his 'Come Back show' or his white 70s suit with the gold studs. None of us could ever visualise how he would look in just six short years and that shortly after that he would be dead. It was a good job we could not see into the future.

As it was, all most people thought of was the present. I was thinking of the immediate future and my Admin Course, which would be just next week.

Coincidentally, I had received a letter from Lyn, who informed me that she had taken the plunge and was also due to go to Spitalgate for Recruit Training in November.

"I've done it Ratty," she wrote, "never thought I would…. Couldn't do WRAF Admin though," she went on to say, "I'm sticking to the old secretarial work."

"Coward!" I wrote back. Whether I would bump into her at Spitalgate would be another matter. I knew that the Recruits were kept well away from those on the WRAF Admin Course.

There was one final thing before my posting from Northwood. My last weekend at Northwood coincided with Remembrance Day so I, and a few of the others, arranged to go into London for the Parade and Service at the War Memorial. I had a much more grown up understanding of the war since my Nijmegen Marches and seeing all the graves at Arnhem and Groesbeek. Even at the tender age of 21 the sight of all those graves brought a tear to my eye. Now, ten years on, we were so near to London and it was easy to just go on the train. We all decided to go in uniform. For one thing we were proud of our best blues, especially on this special day, but also everyone said that we would get a much better chance of getting a good view.

Eventually there were six of us who went – tThe three girls from my room and Betty and Maggie's boyfriends plus me. Also there were quite a few from Northwood taking part in the march past and also some of the sailors from HMS Warrior. We arrived really quite early and it was a good job we did. Even as early as 9.30 a.m. the streets were teaming with people. We walked down past the Houses of Parliament and managed to edge our way along Whitehall and take up a position near to where the Royal Party and the Government Representatives would exit from before taking their places around the Cenotaph. In fact, we were actually ushered to good positions. I think some people thought we were part of the proceedings instead of just onlookers like everybody else! It was a good job we had stout legs because there was a lot of standing about. Already though the massed bands were playing and it really stirred the soul to hear them.

"Look at that," said Betty, and pointed upwards to the Balcony where the Queen Mother would surely be in a little while. "I am sure I saw the curtains move."

"She is looking down on you," I laughed. "She is making sure you are behaving yourself."

Generally speaking there wasn't all that much security. Of course there were the Police lining the route and the military, but that was about it. If there was anybody hiding from view then they were doing just that, because we couldn't see them.

The Band had been playing rousing wartime songs but then suddenly the music changed and the Clergy appeared, preceded by the Choir. Then Edward Heath and all the ministers from the opposition parties. Finally we saw the Queen and the Duke of Edinburgh with Prince Charles and Princess Anne. I looked up at the Balcony and sure enough there were the diminutive figures of The Queen Mum and Princess Margaret. All was set for the service and for the laying of the poppy wreaths.

I had either seen or listened to the Remembrance Day Service ever since I was born. At first it was on the radio, then, when I was old enough, I was dragged along to the local memorial and finally with the introduction of television we had religiously watched it as a family every year. This though was the first time I had seen it in the flesh as it were and all of us from Northwood found it to be a very humbling experience.

With the formal proceedings over we watched as the mood changed again and the march past began. Hundreds and hundreds of men and women from all the armed services marching along to tunes such as 'Long Way to Tipperary' and 'Pack up your Troubles'. First the Navy contingents, then the Army and then all the RAF followed by such as the WVS and Nursing and the blind from St Dunstans and of course the Chelsea Pensioners. It put me in mind of the last five miles of the Nijmegen March but without the gladioli. Slowly the sea of red around the Cenotaph got bigger and bigger as the ushers ran out and took the poppy wreaths and laid them on the steps. Eventually it was all over, though at times we thought it would go on for ever, but when the last contingent had marched past so we followed it down the road and round to Horse Guards where everyone was dispersed. Meanwhile, no doubt, the Royal Family were already indoors having their Sunday Lunch.

Then, just as we were about to make our way to the nearest Wimpey Bar for a sit down and a bite to eat, we were accosted by a Group of Chelsea Pensioners. One of the old boys put his hand on Maggie's arm and with tears in his eyes said, "well done lass, well done, you were all a credit to the youth of today."

With that, they toddled off. None of us had the nerve to tell him that we were not even in it!

The following day I went home for a couple of days leave before taking the train to Grantham in Lincolnshire and my eventual training at RAF Spitalgate and the WRAF Admin Course, not forgetting, of course, the dreaded fortnights Physical Training Course at RAF St. Athan!

The chuckles from my brothers were still ringing in my ears.

"You? On a Physical Training Course? Goodness me, the WRAF must be hard up!"

I just hoped my endeavours on the main Admin Course would be more than sufficient to compensate for my failings in the sport department!

◆ ◆ ◆

~ CHAPTER VII ~

'They Are Just Laundry Marks'

To say it was a rotten day when I arrived at Spitalgate again would be the understatement of the year. I thought back to my first day at Wilmslow which was in July. It had been the hottest day on record and we all thought we were going to melt. Now it was pouring with rain and howling wind. There were a few poor souls walking around, but most people seemed to keep out of the way in classrooms or NAAFI.

A very nice SP on the gate directed me to where I had to go and I made my way to the upstairs room in Welsh Block. Most of the girls who were to be on my Course had arrived and were milling around getting themselves unpacked. All of course were like me, totally devoid of any badges of rank. All except one, that is. I noticed a raincoat draped over a chair with some very smart Corporal tapes on the sleeve.

"Oh that's Jean's," said a little dark girl who had followed my gaze. "By the way, I am Marie."

"Joan," I replied, but most people call me Ratty.

"Jean is a remuster," said another girl. She was a blonde girl and looked about the same age as me. In fact, all the girls were over twenty one and there were a number who, as it eventually turned out, were in their late twenties. I wondered about this Jean who was remustering. Apparently she had popped down to the NAAFI Shop for something but she had stayed in the WRAF and had remustered from Photographic and therefore was already a Corporal. Bells were already starting to ring in my head.

Then the door opened and the object of our conversation entered the room. She stopped in her tracks when she saw me and I just stood there with my mouth gaping open while everyone looked on interestedly. The bells had been right.

"Jean Lawrie..." I gasped, and ran up to give her a big hug. "What the devil are you doing here?"

"I could ask the same of you?" said Jean. "The last I saw of you was when you were leaving the WRAF Block at Rheindahlen never to be seen again."

This was none other than Jean who had been one of the five girls who had been with me on my first Nijmegen March when we had marched with the mixed RAF Germany team. I couldn't believe it. She was quite a bit older than me and must be at least thirty-five now and, yes, she had worked in the Photographic Department in the Big House where I had worked as a Short-hand Typist. She had been one of the few of us who never got into trouble and always behaved herself because she was also in the Salvation Army and she behaved accordingly, like a lady. Unlike the rabble she had to live with in the WRAF Block. Nevertheless we all had got on very well with Jean and it was a delight to see her again. She was as Scottish as haggis and seeing her again brought back so many memories of the march.

I sat on the bed with her and she told me what she had been up to. Seemingly, the promotion prospects in the Photographic Department were less than good and she had got as far as she was likely to go, having received her Corporal stripes some years ago. She had long since made up her mind that the WRAF was going to be her life's career and so had decided to remuster because there was a better chance of promotion in Admin. If she passed the Course OK – and there was no doubt that she would – she would be a Sergeant in no time with a possibility of her Flight Sergeant not too far away. I thought of Payne. Crikey, she had gone from a Corporal in 1959 to a Flight Sergeant when I had last seen her just this year.

"How do you fancy doing the PTI Course?" I laughed. I knew that Jean was not much better than me when it came to sport despite being able to march 100 miles with virtually no blisters.

"Och, I don't fancy it at all," said Jean. "I just hope they will be kind to us, that's all."

There were thirteen of us on the Course and pretty soon we were unpacked and had got to know who was who. I had already met Marie, and then there was a Sandy and another Jean as well as a Paddy and a Helen. It was a job to keep up with all the names straight away but I knew we would all get to know each other in the fullness of time. There were two who were doing the course because they were going into the Police and it was part of the training for them.

We were joined by Sergeant Williams, who was in charge of our Course, and she told us that our first job in the morning would be a kit inspection, just to make sure we had all got everything.

I looked around at the beds where the kit would be laid out. The Block was very different from a Billet but we still had the same stripy bedspreads. I wondered if they had been saved from Wilmslow because they certainly looked no different. However, the pictures on the wall and the flowery curtains were about as far away from my old recruit training station as you could get.

"Right," said Sergeant Williams, "now I need you to get lined up outside and march to the Mess for a meal." Gone was all the shouting that I had grown used to at Wilmslow and then again on the Recruit Training Course. We were actually being treated like adult ladies, probably because we were future potential NCOs and in Jean's case she would be a Senior NCO while the rest of us were still getting used to the laundry marks on our arms. Jean had clearly had her tapes for a few years. However, I had been in before so I got chosen to wear the white band on my arm of the Course Leader. We would each take it in turns on a weekly basis.

We all put on our working blue uniform and went downstairs, lined up outside and then marched to the mess.

"Cor, this is a bit of de-ja-vu!" said Marie.

I thought about Lyn and wondered if I would see her. I did get a letter from her saying that she was due to start at Spitalgate this week on the Recruit Training Course. However, if she had been there I did not have any chance to see because the Sergeant ushered us to our own little section and kept us totally segregated from the Recruits.

"You can't mix with people that you could be in charge of in six months' time," she said.

She had a point.

We got to know each other a bit more over the staple diet of egg and chips and I had longer to chat to Jean. She had been all over the place since leaving Rheindahlen but there had been no chance of promotion.

"How about Flight Sergeant Payne?" I said. "Was she still there when you left?"

"Oh yes, but I think she was due a posting, there was talk of her going to Kinloss."

We finished our meal and then wandered back individually to the Block to get changed and find out more about what we would be doing the next day. It turned out that we were to have a kit inspection to make sure we had everything and those that hadn't were to make a trip to stores.

The kit had changed slightly since our day. No longer were the ladies issued with passion killers and in fact the PE kit had changed completely. Gone were the Air Force blue almost knee-length skirts. They were replaced with very smart white pleated skirts that would have been fully at home at Wimbledon.

"Blimey, this is different," I said to Jean as we opened up the packages and held them against ourselves. "Do you think it will make me any better at PE though?"

We also received black holdalls in addition to our handbags so that we could carry any paperwork or kit around with us. Slowly, I was beginning to feel the part.

The floor still shone like glass because of all the efforts of the last WRAF Admin Course but we knew that we would have to have many Bull nights so nobody wore shoes in the billet and most of us already had the trick of walking around with cloths on our feet in order to keep the floor buffed up. It was a very shiny billet that we left behind that morning to begin our first full day.

We were just about ready for anything and we lined up outside again, this time with one difference. As I was in charge this week it would be me giving the orders and marching them to the classroom. They all lined up in front of me, one or two thinking it was all highly amusing. Marie fumbled about in her handbag and brought out an Instamatic camera.

"Hey Ratty, take a picture of us – we are going to be the best WRAF Admin Course ever."

I stood on the steps of the WRAF Block and attempted to take the picture.

"Come on Ratty!" muttered Iris, a red haired girl who looked as though she would be very good at PE. "Get on with it."

Only Jean actually stood properly to attention, with her head and eyes to the front and her Corporal's stripes on her arm.

"Don't worry everyone," laughed Iris, "we will have Corporal stripes soon."

"Not if you don't pass the course," I gently reminded her.

"Ah, yours will be just laundry marks," laughed Jean. "It took me ten years."

"Don't know what kept you," giggled Dot.

I took the picture and we were joined by the Sergeant, who had been standing just behind me.

"I promise you airwomen," she said in a tone that meant business, "by the time you leave here you will certainly feel you have earned your stripes."

The Admin Course (Jean Lawrie – front row, 2ⁿᵈ from left.)

We decided that the frivolity had better stop and I shouted, "Right turn, by the left quick march!" and we were on our way to our first lesson. We didn't need the Sergeant. We knew where to go and it was my job to lead the way.

We marched down the road between the blocks and saw another flight coming towards us, all in civvies but with their lace up shoes. They were being led by an officious looking Corporal. She put me in mind of Corporal Payne. They were all over the place and Marie and Sandy tried to smother their laughter. Then I spotted Lyn. All my discipline went out through the window.

"Yoo-hoo, Lyn, Lyn!" I shouted. She saw me and waved back.
"Ratty!"

The little Corporal leading the hapless B Flight was quite furious. I got a glower.

"That's not the way for a prospective NCO to behave," she snarled. Then she turned on her flight.

"Head and eyes to the front!" she screamed.

"Oh my gawd!" I thought. "This is a good start!"

Meanwhile the Admin Course had continued marching. They knew where they had to go. I thought that being humble would be my best bet.

"I am so sorry Corporal!" I sounded like Uriah Heap. "We were together the first time round back in 1960 and have kept in touch ever since." I didn't want her taking it out on Lyn.

When she realised that I had been in before she softened a bit.

"You should know better airwoman. Now get on your way."

I felt like saluting but she was only a Corporal and probably hadn't done as many years as I had, and certainly not as many as Jean.

I caught up with the rest of my Course as they were just filing into the classroom. Sergeant Williams had not been messing about when she told us we would earn our tapes. From that moment on our feet did not touch the ground.

◆ ◆ ◆

"Now airwoman, I have reason to believe you are pregnant."

"No, no, no!" shouted the WRAF Sergeant who was taking our lesson. "You can't accuse an airwoman of being pregnant. You have to get them to tell you."

"That's easier said than done." I whispered to Jean, who was sitting next to me.

We had all been given bits of paper with 'scenarios' on to act out. At the moment it was Paddy pretending to be an NCO while Helen was the poor airwoman pretending to be pregnant. She was also under instructions to be as awkward as she could possibly be.

"I've had complaints from your Section that you have been late in for work and have felt sick," persevered Paddy.

"Oh, it was probably something I had eaten," replied Helen.

"But you have put on so much weight!" continued Paddy.

"I know Corporal," smiled Helen, being as awkward as possible, "I really will have to diet."

We all started to snigger and the Sergeant let them battle it out for a while just to show them.

"Now you can see what you might be up against," she said. "If somebody doesn't want to tell you they are pregnant then you have to coax it out of them like this." She turned to Helen.

"Young lady, is there something you wish to tell me?"

"No!" replied Helen, still acting.

"Well, let me put it as plainly as possible," sneered our tutor. "If there is something I should know and further down the line I find out you have been lying to me, I'll put you on a charge."

Nothing had changed, in that respect, since 1959 and before. If an airwoman got herself pregnant, that was her ticket out of the WRAF immediately. For all sorts of reasons there were always those who did not want to admit it until they were forced to but, I learned very quickly, that Admin were very much governed by human rights and you couldn't accuse without very good grounds.

We all had different scenarios to act out which might crop up during the working day of an Admin Corporal and although, some of the time, it was done with laughter, the actual lesson was deadly serious.

Funnily enough my task was to quiz a couple of girls who had been caught coming back into the Block late and drunk. This was certainly a case of 'de-ja-vu' when I think of the number of times we had run the gauntlet of WRAF Admin the first time around.

And so it went on, from classroom to parade ground and then back to classroom again, and then there was the dreaded Gym.

"Well, at least this is a bit better than what we were issued with at Wilmslow," said Jean, holding up her smart white pleated skirt. We certainly looked capable of being sporty when we all made our way to the Gym that afternoon, but looks aren't everything – not in my case anyway. No amount of fancy white sports outfits would make a PTI out of me. It was all right for the young fit ones, but Jean and I, despite our several Nijmegen

Marches, were not in the same league as some of them. The gym was huge and just seemed to be a mass of badminton nets and ghastly gym equipment that looked like instruments of torture to me. The Corporal PTI who had the unenviable job of taking charge of us was slim, fit and very brown. She didn't look as though she had an ounce of excess fat underneath her black trousers and white top.

"Come on, a run round the Gym first," she called out, "come on, keep up!"

Gawd! I could still taste my dinner.

We all did a steady jog behind her, like ducks following their mother. Well, not quite 'all'. Jean and I puffed and panted a reasonable distance behind. I couldn't help feeling that she had been well briefed on the fact that she had two 'old dears' in the group, who had seen better days, because she was really quite considerate. Too considerate for my liking.

"That's it you two – you are doing well."

'Liar!' I thought.

Afterwards we all had to play some badminton or squash which wasn't too bad because then we could go at our own pace. We got beaten of course, but at least it was at our own pace.

We managed to get most of the drill out on the parade square despite the time of year, but when it was really blowing a gale or raining, then we went into the big hangar where every sound echoed and was magnified a hundred times. Within ten minutes I had a headache with the echoing of the feet on the floor and the sound of the shouting. It was much nicer on the parade square and I began to wish I had been there in the summer as I had been at Wilmslow.

It was all different now though. Now, we had to be taught to teach drill. Well I had done it before with the cadets although I had received help from the ATC. Now we had scripts to learn and there was a script for each drill movement that we had to learn by heart and we each had to take a turn at being the instructor.

"Watch my demonstration," I barked, trying to remember my script. "Listen to my explanation and pay attention. Flight... stand at ease."

The Admin Course dutifully stood at ease under the watchful eye of Sergeant Williams.

"Can you all see me?" I shouted. They all shuffled around so that they could.

"Can you all hear me?" I tried to remember it word for word. Of course I knew what to do, it was just the words that took the remembering.

"About turn!" I demonstrated, following my own instruction while the group watched.

"About turn by numbers, one pause two."

"One – on the command 'one' a turn is made through 180 degrees on the heel of the right foot and the toe of the left foot."

"By numbers – two," I went on, safe in the knowledge that I had their attention.

"Bend the knee and bring it forward to the position of attention."

I turned to face them.

"You will now practice this movement by numbers by calling out the numbers - Flight – Attention! About turn – by numbers – flight one – by numbers – flight two."

They all successfully about turned and I was rewarded with a round of applause from Sergeant Williams.

"Good lord" I thought, "what the devil is it going to be like to learn the about turn on the march, or march past in review order?"

Over the next few weeks I certainly found out!

◆ ◆ ◆

By the time we got to the end of the day we were all knackered but it didn't end there. We still had the Bull Night – or Domestic Night as it was now called – and we still had the continual kit inspections. There seemed to be no respite. With Christmas

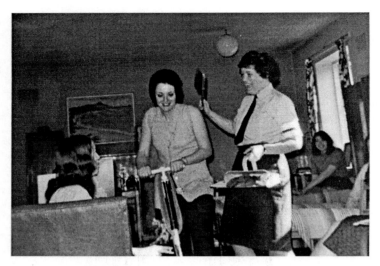

Domestic Night – Admin Course. Me with the dustpan.

looming it was as if they wanted to get the whole Course done and dusted before the break with little regard for the fact that we had another couple of months when we came back. It didn't stop the usual tom-foolery though – that hadn't changed over the years and quite often the Domestic Night finished in us all dissolving into laughter as we acted the fool with each other.

The beauty was though that we could use an electric polisher. Gone were the days of the bumper – a sort of swinging brick on the end of a pole that we used to polish the floor.

"You don't know how lucky you are," said Jean one evening when Dot and Marie were moaning about yet another Domestic Night. "You should try it in a billet. We had awful stoves to black lead and there were twenty-eight of us to a room."

"Oh, here we go again," Laughed Dot. "You will be telling me next that you supped by candlelight and did your washing with stones."

"Not quite as bad as that," I replied, sensing an opportunity to back Jean up and tease them at the same time. "But we did have to whiten the coke and cut the grass with nail scissors."

For a minute they all believed me. It wasn't quite true but I did know some of the blokes that had to do that as a punishment.

"Jean's right," I went on, "it's a different world now."

I remembered my recruit training at Wilmslow with fondness though. We did work hard but we had some laughs there too. Now it was like the lap of luxury to have the toilets and bathrooms in the same Block and not to have to have a half mile walk down some stone passage to a bath that didn't have a plug. Wilmslow was about to be closed when we were there and it was being run down, whereas Spitalgate was all spanking new. The discipline hadn't changed though. Even without Corporal Payne, it was still pretty rigid. I got to wondering what had happened to her. I had visions of turning a corner and coming face to face with her, but so far it hadn't happened. The latest I heard was that she was in Cyprus and then somebody said that she had gone to Kinloss. Well, just so long as I didn't go to either of those places then everything would be OK.

The chances of seeing anything of Lyn were absolutely zilch. Occasionally I saw her heading for the NAAFI and once I got a note from her that had been put in with the post. *'Sorry Ratty,'* it said. *'Us mortals are not allowed to mix with you lot.'*

I knew we would stay in touch though and she was due to have her Passing Out Parade and leave long before I had finished my Course.

Before we knew it Christmas was upon us and it was time to go home for a few days. It was lovely to go home, of course, but in some ways I wished the Course had gone straight through and I could get it over and done with.

By now both my brothers were courting strong and my mother was full of the sounds of wedding bells. They kept her busy that year as it wasn't just them but their girlfriends as well.

Nice girls who I soon got to know and love. Of course they were big grown up men now. Richard was twenty and Mick was twenty-four. Richard had been just eight when I had joined up for the first time. It didn't seem possible. Where had the time gone? Now we had Carol and Pamela as additions to our family.

Of course everyone wanted to know when I would be getting my Corporals tapes and when I would be showing them off.

"It's all very well," I told them, "but they are just laundry marks really – I'm not going to be paid for them straight away."

I knew though that my Dad was very proud of me. It reminded him of his own time in the RAF which of course had been wartime. I would have to go some to catch up with him though. He was a Flight Sergeant when he came out and an acting Warrant Officer, and they certainly were not laundry marks. They were the result of active service in France, Malta and Egypt.

We had a lovely family Christmas with the usual turkey and trimmings and then settled down as we had as a family for every year since 1953 to listen to the Queen's Speech. Who knows where I would be next Christmas. I hoped it would be right here.

◆◆◆

It was a long and arduous journey back up to Lincolnshire and the already leaden sky was full of the promise of some snow. In fact when I got off the train and made my way back to camp there was quite a film of it on the ground. With a good three months of the Course left to do I still found myself wondering if I had done the right thing. But, as I began to meet up with other girls on their way back from Christmas Grant I knew that there was nothing to beat the comradeship that the uniform invokes. Of course, those on the Recruit Training Courses were in civvies as they were not allowed to wear their best blues until their Passing Out Parades but those of us on the Admin Course and many of the permanent staff travelled in the uniform they were so proud of. There was a friendly wave from the 'snowdrops' in the Guardroom and I picked my way gingerly along the road to the Block. The ground was really quite slippery now.

"Way-hay!" cried Paddy as I entered the room, "about time Ratty."

Of course the Scottish girls were not very happy because they were missing New Year at home but it couldn't be helped.

"You can tell it's an English WRAF," said a disgruntled Sandy, "Sassenachs!"

Jean, also Scots of course, never got upset at anything.

"Don't worry Sandy," she soothed, "you can enjoy New Year again."

"Huh!" Sandy picked up her beetle crushers and started polishing them furiously. After all, there was yet another kit inspection the following morning.

It wasn't just any old kit inspection. It was the inspection by one of the Flight Commanders in readiness for a further inspection later that week by the Commanding Officer herself – none other than the Air Commodore. To misquote the great Sir Winston Churchill – 'never had so many shoes been polished and re-polished by so few'.

Well at least there was less kit now. We didn't have to put out underclothes or stockings and gone were the passion killers.

We were up at the crack of dawn and went to breakfast and then came back and busied ourselves getting it all ready. I looked round the room and it all looked perfect with every bedspread aligned with the stripes lined up with each other and bed stacks like large perfect liquorice allsorts. Everyone stood back so proud of their efforts. That is, we were until Dot shattered our dreams of perfection.

"Oh my God, where has *that* come from?"

She held up her pristine white PE shirt and it had a blue biro smudge right on the front of it.

"You silly cow!" cried Marie. "What are you doing with a biro near your shirt?"

"I haven't," cried Dot. "I genuinely do not know where that has come from."

"Well you can't do anything much about it now," I said.

Suddenly, it was Jean who came to the rescue. She had been rifling around in her washing bag and came out with a tube of white toothpaste.

"You won't get away with that!" I laughed.

"It's all we have got," said Jean. She carefully smoothed the white paste over the biro mark. It worked just so long as nobody looked too closely. We had three PE shirts so Dot put the offending one right on the bottom with the others overlapping the stain. We all crossed our fingers and hoped for the best, just as the Sergeant and the Inspecting Officer strode into the room.

As it happened it was Dot who was Course Leader this week.

"Room, room Attention!" she shouted, still wondering where the offending blue mark had come from.

Sergeant Williams picked up a shoe here, and inspected a bed stack there but all in all she just walked around the room, knowing, or thinking she knew, that these were airwomen who knew already how to lay out a kit inspection. Thankfully Dot got away with it.

"For goodness sake go and get another one from stores before the CO's inspection." I said. "You won't get away with it twice."

Two days later the lady herself came round with an entourage of Junior and Senior NCOs. She wasn't so bad though and just strolled around trying to look interested in our shiny shoes and neatly pressed shirts. The inspection with Sergeant Williams had been more unnerving, to say the least.

They still kept us separated from the Recruits as if we were lepers but I did manage to meet Lyn eventually. She managed to get a note to me to suggest we meet up at the Church Club. *"Honestly"* she wrote *"it's like trying to meet a flippin' boyfriend behind the bike sheds."*

I couldn't stay long because they really were making us earn our tapes on the Admin Course and I had some studying to do, but it was long enough for her to tell me that she had been posted to Brampton. She would not be coming back here because she had chosen to stay in her same trade of shorthand typist and needed very little trade training.

"We had better be careful," I laughed, "meeting up like this – we will have people thinking we are a couple of queers."

One thing had not changed since 1959. It was still an offence for people to have a relationship with the same sex and the word 'gay' had not been invented yet. This was also part of our learning curve on the Admin Course.

I was sorry not to see her Passing Out Parade but we would not be given the time off to do that. But I wasn't too worried. I would remain in touch with her, just the same as I had remained in touch with Pat Seymour and June and Jan from my first time in the WRAF. I wished her goodbye and good luck and made my way back through the thin layer of snow to the Block.

"Cheerio!" she shouted behind me, "and good luck on that PE course."

She laughed as I put two fingers up.

◆ ◆ ◆

~ CHAPTER VIII ~

'A Silk Purse Out of a Sow's Ear'

I f I thought the period before Christmas on my Admin Course was the worst over, then I was sadly mistaken. There were drill scripts to learn, more kit inspections as if we hadn't had enough and masses of RAF History and the do's and don'ts of how to handle the young women who would be in our care. Then of course there was the drill and the dreaded PE, though, to be fair the PTIs were quite tolerant of Jean and I and just giggled gently between themselves as we brought up the rear whenever we were out running.

"Och, this is a bit different from the Nijmegen March," grunted Jean as we did the circuit of the Gym for the umpteenth time. We had been lapped more than once by the fit young things on the Course. I couldn't answer her for I had no breath left, but certainly I would have much sooner been marching.

Suddenly there was a squeal and all the ones who had just overlapped us were toppling over each other as somebody lost their footing. It was Iris.

"Ouch, oh my God, that is painful," she yelled, as everybody crowded round.

"Out of the way, out of the way, stand back!" The PTI was there like a rocket while we watched Iris's ankle swell up before our eyes. She was in agony. For some reason her ankle had given way and she had fallen over on it with all her weight and had clearly cracked a bone. The young girl who was in charge of us today for Physical Training ran to the office on the side of the gym and phoned sick quarters and within minutes the medics arrived carrying a stretcher. There would be no more Gym for Iris today or for many more days.

In fact, as it turned out, her ankle was so bad that she was unable to complete the Course and it was arranged for her to go back to her old station and await another Course which she would join half way though once it was healed.

"Well, at least I will probably be here in the summer!" she said, as she packed her bags and hobbled around on a crutch, saying goodbye to people. She was putting on a brave face but she was thoroughly fed up and we were now down to twelve.

◆ ◆ ◆

We packed a lot into January, and in early February it would be the long awaited fortnight on the PTI Course. But first I had a pair of passion killers to get rid of. I was determined I was going to leave them at Spitalgate somewhere but I wasn't going to take the chance of hauling them up the flagpole. I got the opportunity one evening when it was quite dark. Dot and I were coming back from the NAAFI and I had the knickers in my pocket just in case a chance should present itself. We were just about to turn our corner to go into our block when I spotted that the flower bed had recently been turned over and weeded where daffodil bulbs were starting to poke through. There was hardly anybody about as most people were either in the Blocks doing the usual polishing and bulling, or they were in the NAAFI. We were only on our way back because we wanted to get our packing done ready to move on.

"Hey Dot," I whispered, "keep an eye open for me!"

"What!" cried the person who was about to become an RAF Policewoman. "What are you up to?"

"Just keep watch, I'll explain afterwards."

I crept over to the flower bed and, sure enough, the ground was very soft and I could move it with my hands without disturbing the bulbs that were planted in groups. I laid the passion killers to rest. With a bit of luck the flowers would grow up around them. They'd had a good innings having been to Hereford, Medmenham, Rheindahlen, Northwood and back and forth between me and Pat. They deserved to be left in peace among the flowers.

"Blimey!" said Dot. "Good job nobody saw us."

The following day we all got our results from our overall performances during the Course. These took in the Drill and RAF History, Kit Inspections and all the other Administration duties. As would be expected, and hoped for, Jean came top and I came second. After all Jean had never left the WRAF and I was a re-entrant – it would have been embarrassing if it had been otherwise. Dot came third but, to us, she was top of those that did not have Jean's and my advantages. It was just as well that we did well here at Spitalgate. We both knew that from now on it would be downhill all the way.

That was it, next on the Agenda would be transport to Llanwrst on the outskirts of Snowdonia in North Wales and with a bit of luck we would be on our Permanent Stations before the end of the month.

"Oh gawd, here we go," I said to Jean, "this is going to be a laugh a minute."

◆ ◆ ◆

"Cor, he is a bit nice!" whispered Dot, as we got off the bus at RAF Llanwrst and met our Instructor for the first time. He was a PTI Sergeant and very, very nice looking. He soon had us eating out of his hand, but no matter how gorgeous he was there would be nothing that would bring sport to me naturally.

Llanwrst was a very small station within a short distance of the foothills of Snowdon. It was dedicated to RAF Outdoor Activities and we were to be here for a few days before going south to RAF St Athan for our Physical Training. We did manage to find the time to take a walk into the little village nearby, where we found a nice fish and chip shop but then it was back to our rooms in the wooden outbuildings for our last few hours before the torture began. Our Instructors didn't lose any time. On the first morning, after breakfast, we were given life jackets and taken to the nearby river for canoeing.

"They are having a laugh!" I said to Jean."The last time I went canoeing was at Medmenham and then I nearly tipped the ruddy thing up."

The handsome PTI who we soon found out was called Dave Taylor looked across at me.

"Don't worry, I won't let you drown," he twinkled.

"I wouldn't mind him giving me the kiss of life," said Paddy.

We all stood on the bank and watched as he and a young female PTI, who looked as though she had been born with muscles, got in one of the canoes that were all lined up in a row and proceeded to demonstrate how to turn the thing over on one side until they were almost in the water and you could see the bottom of the boat sticking up in the air facing us.

"You are bloody joking!" said Dot. I could feel myself turning white.

"It's OK – have a go anyway, just don't let any water in the canoe."

We were all helped into our canoes, some in pairs and others in single man boats. I was quite happy, sort of, to paddle around near to the bank but the very idea of turning the boat on its side was not for me. I watched as some of the braver ones had a go. Apart from anything else it was February and freezing cold.

"Come on Ratcliff, your turn," shouted Sgt Taylor. "Don't be a wimp."

I gingerly put the oar in the water and leaned the boat over but nowhere near far enough for the Sergeant. Well that was the first PTI test we had failed. Good job we had both done well in the main, and most important, part of our Course back at Spitalgate. I paddled around for a while trying to look clever. I still had the task of getting out of the thing yet. Bit by bit I edged it towards the bank and the Sergeant managed to lean across and pull at the bow of the canoe and hold it steady while I almost fell out of it onto the bank. He hadn't finished with me though. I think he was beginning to think it was all a big joke because his next wheeze was to put me in a canoe with Jean! I got in the back and then had Jean's bottom in my face as she scrambled to get in the front. All this time the rest of the class were either on the bank or in canoes watching our antics and laughing.

"Gawd Jean!" I yelled, "steady on, you are rocking the thing." I held on for grim death as the boat rocked from side to side and then steadied. Then we were off, with me trying to keep in time with her.

"Get it together!" yelled the handsome Sergeant, as we struggled with our oars. We started to ship water and I shouted at Jean.

"Steady on mate!"

All she wanted to do was to get it over and done with and she was canoeing as if her life depended on it. I watched in horror as more water entered the canoe and we went round in circles.

"Come on Jean," I cried, "I think our time is up – left hand down a bit!" By now everybody was in stitches with laughing. It was like something out of an old Laurel and Hardy movie. I was Laurel and Jean was Hardy. There was quite a strong current but we did make it right to the bank just as the canoe sank from under us with the weight of the water we had shipped. We were able to scramble up the bank and some of the hardier PTIs rescued the boat and Jean's oar that had gone floating off somewhere. I was still holding mine.

"Well, that's the bloody last time I am ever going canoeing!" I declared, amid all the laughter. "They had better not post me to a Station with no PTI, that's all I can say, otherwise the air force is really in trouble."

"Never mind ladies," laughed the Sergeant, "a spot of mountaineering for you tomorrow."

"What!" I gasped "You are joking?"

Actually, I did know that we would be doing some sort of climbing because we had already been issued with some special climbing shoes but I had put it to the back of my mind in the hope that it would go away.

"You are not going to try and make us climb up Mount Snowdon?" I gasped. "You have got no chance!"

"Well, you never know," he grinned, "just you wait and see." The very remarkably fit young PTI girls who had just joined us laughed in merriment. They thought it was all very amusing.

"Don't worry," said one particularly brown and fit-looking young girl. "He is just winding you up. You will only be doing the foothills."

"Huh," mumbled Jean, "the word 'only' could be a bit different to somebody as fit as that."

We were pretty fit considering, but some of these PTIs were like Adonis compared to us.

One thing was for sure, we were all ready for our tea when we got back to our quarters and, following yet another check on our kit for the next day, we all made sure we got an early night. After all we really did not know what was in store.

"Well you know what they say?" said Paddy as she pulled the covers over herself, "if you can't take a joke you shouldn't have joined."

◆ ◆ ◆

The following morning I felt like the prisoner who "ate a healthy breakfast" before going to the gallows. We were to leave the handsome Sergeant behind and this time we would have a very young, but also handsome RAF PTI Corporal to lead the way. We were to be taken to our starting point in an old RAF lorry. I felt even more as though I was going to my doom as we all piled in the back. Someone took a picture and I looked as grim as I felt.

We were dropped off in the foothills of Snowdon but it might just as well have been Everest as far as I was concerned.

In the back of the lorry. I'm in the middle of the centre row.

"Right, come on!" cried the enthusiastic young Corporal. "We can be there and back in time for tea." Already most of the girls were striding on ahead.

Now I have done many a Nijmegen March, nearly all of which takes place on flat ground. True, even the Dutch managed to find us a few hills on the third day but nothing like what we were expected to do now. I looked up and the area we were supposed to climb might just as well have been Everest. It seemed to stretch onwards and upwards for ever. It wasn't really mountain climbing because it was more hill walking but these hills were not lovely lush green grass. They were full of slate and stones which moved and crunched under your feet. I seemed to take two steps forward and one step back. It wasn't long before Jean and I were falling behind the rest and our Corporal had to work overtime as he came backwards and forwards between us and the main group. Within half an hour we were both totally puffed out.

"Cor, this is not like Nijmegen is it Jean?" I puffed, as I stopped for the umpteenth time and caught my breath.

On the plus side, the scenery was breath-taking. You could see right across the valley and the sea right in the distance. But we really were not being given much of a chance to appreciate it. We both sat down on the slates and watched the tail end of the rest of the girls disappearing into the distance. Clearly they knew where they were going.

"You can't sit there!" said the Corporal "I have to catch the others up." So we pulled ourselves up and trundled onwards again. And this was only a foothill? What the devil was the real thing like? I could remember quite clearly when Hilary and Tensing conquered the top of Everest for the first time way back in 1953. Now I could start to grasp their achievement. They had done more than we had done before they had even left their hotel or whatever it was they stayed in before setting out.

"All you have to do is make it up to the Cairn," said the Corporal.

"Cairn! What's a bloody cairn when it's at home?" I said to Jean.

"It's a pile of stones at the top of a mountain to mark the top," she panted.

I was certainly glad of the stout climbing shoes with studs in that we had been issued with. At least it stopped us slipping. Well, a bit anyway.

At one point we came within sight of a narrow road where cars could drive up.

"Och, will ye look at that!" said Jean, "maybe we can get a lift."

She was only joking but it was very tempting to go and cross to where the road was and thumb a lift. That would fool everybody, if they got to the Cairn and found us waiting there.

I could feel my legs stinging and I was sure I was getting a blister. We could still see one or two of the stragglers in the distance and spot the figure of our Corporal as he left us and made his way towards them. Higher and ever higher we went. At one point I started to wonder if we really were on Snowdon itself and that he had not been kidding us. Eventually though our climb did start to reach its end and we could see the summit and all the girls gathered round at the top, presumably at this aforementioned Cairn, in the distance.

"Nearly there," puffed Jean.

"Thank Gawd," I replied.

Reassured with the idea that we were not lost I sat down again. Most of where we were walking seemed to consist of slate and gravel but there were bits of grass which were still damp with thawing snow. I didn't care, I just sat down and Jean sat beside me and we contemplated the scenery. Most of it was shrouded in a mist but nevertheless it was stunning and though I knew I would not come ten out of ten in mountaineering I was glad that we had made the climb. I thought of my parents and my brothers. They would be amazed.

Jean scrambled to her feet again. "At least we can put all this behind us when we go to St. Athan," she said.

"Absolutely," I replied, as I hauled myself up to my feet. "These flippin' mountain boots can go to a jumble sale, I never want to see them again."

"What will you do if you get to a station with no PTI and you have to take them mountaineering?" she laughed.

"I'd buy myself out!" I said truthfully.

We could hear the cries of the girls egging us onwards and soon we were within reach of them.

There was an enormous cheer from everyone as we reached the top and sunk to our knees. There was the famous Cairn,

At the Cairn.

just a pile of stones, but just for that moment it was the best pile of stones in the world. There was much back slapping and photograph taking.

"Now, all we have to do is climb back down again," said our Corporal, with a twinkle in his eye.

He nearly got pushed off the mountain!

He seemed to be very fond of pulling our legs. We walked away from the Cairn and rounded a series of boulders and there, in the distance, at the top of the road we had seen earlier, was the RAF truck. I could have kissed the driver when we got there.

I climbed in, along with Dot, Sandy, Jean and all the rest. Our Corporal, who we now knew was Brian Carter, climbed in with us and we entertained him to all our old Wilmslow and Spitalgate songs on the way back to Llanwrst. Jean and I, who had been to RAF Wilmslow back in the fifties managed to teach all the younger girls a few songs that even they did not know.

That evening was spent in the local pub and most of us were thoroughly the worse for wear when we crawled back to the accommodation for our last night at Llanwrst. I threw the climbing boots into my haversack and hoped that I would never see them again. Dot was absolutely paralytic and fell onto her bed fully clothed.

"You are all going to regret it in the morning!" said Jean, who had not drunk at all. "Don't forget, we still have the rest of the Course to do and we have that journey down to St Athan."

"Jean!" we all shouted, and she ended up de-bedded on the floor with her mattress on top of her.

She had been right though. There were some very sore heads the following morning and for some of us the sight of bacon and egg for breakfast was all a bit too much. Thinking of the forthcoming bus journey I decided to opt for a cereal and left it at that.

We managed to get ready though and boarded the now familiar RAF bus that would take us down to the Vale of Glamorgan and RAF St Athan. Not for the first time I wondered what on earth had possessed me to re-join the WRAF and in the trade of WRAF Admin of all things.

"Don't worry," said Jean, reading my thoughts, "we will muddle through it together."

The journey passed quite pleasantly, despite the frost on some of the roads, and once the hangovers had lifted we entertained the driver with our WRAF Songs.

"Oh, they say that in the air force the food is might fine,
A crumb fell off the table and killed a pal of mine.
Oh I don't want no more of air force life,
Gee Sarge I wanna go, but they won't let me go,
Gee Sarge I wanna go ho-o-ome!"

I wondered how many times the middle aged RAF driver had heard that in his time driving people back and forth in the bus.

Upon arrival we were booked in and taken to tea, which was just awful. I hadn't tasted such awful food since I was at Rheindahlen in 1961.

"Blimey!" said Sandy, "thank goodness it is only for a week."

We spent much of the next day in the classroom being taught how to referee Netball matches and the rules for playing hockey and cricket. I was quite sure that I would be doing none of these things but I tried to take in such things as 'leg before wicket' and 'silly mid-on'. It was all double Dutch to me.

Then came the running. St Athan was a big camp, not only used for the PTIs but also the Apprentice Training School. Every so often we would see flights of them smartly marching to and fro to their classrooms or to the hangars for their practical engineering work. The PTIs thought it would be highly amusing to run us all round the camp and supply the entertainment for the young lads. I'm sure we looked a vision of loveliness in our white pleated skirts and white tops jogging round the camp in our twos, with Jean and myself panting away in the rear. We did have one very nice WRAF Sergeant who took charge of us. She was older than us but very, very fit and extremely brown and she did not have an ounce of excess flesh on her. We soon learned her name was Pauline Brown and she did have some sympathy for Jean and myself. I had a feeling that she had been pre-warned about us, and she did her best to egg us on.

"Come on, you can do it," she laughed and then shouted to the front of the group. "Hey, slow down a bit, wait for us oldies." I took to her straight away.

Needless to say when it came to the exams Jean and I came bottom of our PTI Course.

"Oh well," I said, "we can't win them all."

"Don't worry," said Pauline, "you came top on your Admin Course and that is what you came in to do. It's just as well you were not coming into the WRAF to be Physical Training Instructors though, otherwise we would have been in trouble."

"You can't make a silk purse out of a sows ear!" I grinned.

Despite our abysmal efforts on the PTI Course we did get our Corporal tapes and by the end of the week stores had sewn them onto all our essential uniform. All that remained now was to get our postings to our permanent stations. It had been little over a year since I had first walked into the Recruiting Centre in London and argued with them as to whether I could keep my old number or not. Such a lot had happened since then that it seemed like a lifetime ago.

"RAF Shawbury?" I exclaimed when I first learned of my posting. "Where the devil is that? Never heard of it."

"It's near Shrewsbury in Shropshire!" Sergeant Brown informed me.

"What a bloomin' mouthful."

"Now there is one very important thing she needs to know," said Dot, who had just come and joined us, having secured a posting to RAF Benson. "Does Shawbury have a PTI?"

"Oh gawd yes!" I panicked, "it had better had!"

The Sergeant laughed. "Don't worry, yes, they do have a very good gym and a PTI to go with it."

I breathed a sigh of relief. I didn't know what it would be like being a fully-fledged WRAF Admin at RAF Shawbury but I didn't care as long as they did have a PTI and there was no Flight Sergeant Payne. There was another thing on the horizon too. I would have to do some negotiating as soon as I arrived there. In July I hoped to be doing the Nijmegen Marches again. I had promised last year that I would take the cadets for one last time before somebody else took over completely. I would have to try and secure the necessary leave. I just hoped that the Senior NCO who I would be working with would be sympathetic.

There were a few tears when we finally said goodbye to each other and made our separate ways to our homes before taking a few days leave. I was fairly lucky as it wasn't too bad to get the train to London and then home to my parents, but for some it was a long journey right up to the north of Scotland and Ireland in a couple of cases.

There were more hugs and cries of "Good luck!" and bit by bit everyone found their trains and it would be unlikely that we would see each other again. I gave Jean an extra big hug. We went back a long way.

"Good luck," I said, "you will be a Sergeant before you know it."

"Good luck," she replied. "Give my love to Nijmegen when you get there!"

"If I get there!"

With that, she was on her train up to Scotland.

◆ ◆ ◆

It was great to be back home again and I felt very proud walking down the road in my uniform with my Corporal stripes on my arm I think my Dad was a bit proud of me too. I glanced towards the sideboard where my Mother had a framed photo of me in uniform that I had taken the first time I was in. It had been taken at Wilmslow when I was eighteen.

"You will have to have a new one to put in that frame now Mum," I said. "One with my tapes on."

"We will put one of you in your tapes somewhere," she said "but I do like that photo, I don't want to change that."

She was right, of course, it was a good photo taken by a professional photographer in my first six weeks in the WRAF, when everything was new and exciting.

Just then my brother Mick arrived in the house with his girlfriend Carol. Already they were engaged and Mum was busy fussing over the forthcoming wedding, which was planned for September. She was a lovely girl who he had met at work and I soon got to know and like her. I made a mental note that as soon as I was sure of the date I must book some leave. More leave and I hadn't even arrived at my new station yet!

"It's going to be the 16th September," said Carol. I couldn't believe it, my baby brother getting married. That wasn't all. Richard, who had been courting his girlfriend Pamela since he was fourteen, also announced that they were to be married in January the following year.

"Gosh Dad," I laughed, "two weddings in the space of four months – good job we were not all girls."

"Well, we have given up waiting for you," smiled Dad.

It was true. It didn't look as though I would be joining them in married life. I still visualised myself as a WRAF Admin Sergeant or even a Flight Sergeant one day.

Most of my friends from the first time round were married now. Pat Seymour had a child and June was married with two little girls. Only Jan and Lyn still remained single, and Lyn was at RAF Brampton.

"Well, you never know what may lie in wait at Shawbury," I laughed.

"Gawd help him," laughed Mick. Nothing had changed but there would be something radically wrong if Mick stopped pulling my leg.

I did have a lovely few days at home and it was great to see them all again. The time came for me to catch the train up to Waterloo all too soon.

Dad offered me a lift to the station but I declined. Even after all these years I still got emotional and upset if someone came and saw me off at the train station. Once I was on my way I was OK. It was just that initial wrench as I saw them fading into the distance as the train pulled away that I didn't like.

"No thanks Dad, I'll walk. It will do me good."

They all saw me off at the door and even then I still had to hold back the tears. This was, or should be, the start of the rest of my life.

~ CHAPTER IX ~

RAF Shawbury

It was still very cold and there was frost on the ground when I arrived at Shawbury in the afternoon at the end of February. I didn't know what to expect as the bus crawled through the open countryside mostly over ungritted roads, but when it pulled up at the Guardroom and I saw the sight of a familiar World War Two aeroplane at the entrance I felt strangely comforted. I could see straight away that the accommodation blocks were on the opposite side of the road to the main station. I struggled up to the Guardroom with my suitcase and kitbag and plonked both on the ground as I fumbled for my F1250 to prove who I was. There were a couple of 'snowdrops' and a 'modplod' trying to look busy. The Modplod (or Ministry of Defence Policeman) to give him his proper name, looked up and smiled in welcome as one of the snowdrops checked his notes to see that I was expected. He was usually used to checking in trainee Air Traffic Controllers because Shawbury was the training school for the people whose job it was to make sure aeroplanes did not bump into each other in the sky.

"Ah, Corporal Ratcliff," he smiled, "welcome to Shawbury. I shall point you in the direction of the WRAF Block in a minute." The sound of somebody calling me Corporal Ratcliff was quite strange and would take some getting used to. He picked up the phone. "I've got your new Corporal here for you Flight," he said. There was more rustling of paper and then he came out of the office and picked up my suitcase. I warmed towards him straight away. Here was a gentleman.

"Thanks," I said, as he ushered me out of the gate and across the road to the first block in front of us.

"This is the WRAF Block," he said. "Flight Sergeant James is inside waiting for you, just go in and turn left." He put my case on the ground. "I dare not go any further," he laughed, "or she will have my giblets."

I walked through the double doors into the hallway with its highly polished floor and turned left down a corridor just as the door right at the end opened and the Flight Sergeant came out to greet me. She was slim with dark hair and glasses. It was very difficult to tell how old she was but I would have said she was in her forties. I dropped my luggage on the floor in the corridor as she held out her hand to shake mine.

"Welcome," she said. "I'm Flight Sergeant James." She opened the door right next to the Admin Office and flung it wide. "This is your room," she said proudly. "You are lucky – you can't swing a cat in the airwomen's rooms."

I poked my head inside and found I had a reasonable sized room and even had my own sink. She then opened the door of the room opposite. "This is the normal room," she said. It was indeed very small, with built in wardrobes and chest and just enough room for a bed and a chair. It seemed that everyone had single rooms. I couldn't help feeling already that I preferred the idea of sharing a room and having the space and the comradeship of each other.

"I know what you are thinking," she said. "We remember billets, don't we?" Clearly she had done her homework about me.

It was still only four o'clock and the Block was virtually empty because all the trainees were at lessons and the permanent staff were at work. She pushed open the door of the Admin Office that she had just emerged from and it opened on to a very large room with her desk dominating the middle and mine to one side. I could see that already there was a heap of paperwork waiting for me. She caught my glance.

"Oh, don't worry about that," she said, "go and unpack and get your bed made – by then it will be time to go to tea anyway."

Even as she was speaking I could hear the double doors opening and shutting as airwomen started to come back to the Block. Many, though, would go straight to tea.

"I'll get Corporal Frazer to take you to tea," she said. "You get unpacked."

I didn't know who Corporal Frazer was, of course, but she disappeared back into the office and made a phone call.

I looked around me. Well, certainly I wouldn't have far to go to work. Goodness me, my office was just on the other side of the wall. I could knock on the door of the Admin Office without leaving my own doorway. It was a decent size though and somebody had kindly seen to it that I had a nice neat bed stack at the head of the bed. By the time I had finished unpacking and hanging my uniform up Corporal Frazer arrived down the corridor. She was slim, dark and very fit looking because she was a PTI. She looked very smart in her PTI trousers with a white open necked blouse under her battle dress top. Following close behind her was another Corporal in normal working blue uniform.

"Hello," said Corporal Frazer, "I'm Barbara, and this is my friend Betty Carter." As they were introducing themselves the Flight Sergeant locked the office door and disappeared down the corridor.

"Cheerio!" she called. "Don't be late for work in the morning will you? After all, you have all of two yards to go!" With that she was gone.

"Come on," said Barbara, "leave all that until later – come and have some tea."

I was still in my best blue uniform, so I just plonked my hat back on my head and followed the two of them meekly across the road to the Mess, which was already buzzing with activity. They found a table where other junior NCOs were sitting and then we lined up to go and help ourselves to whatever was on offer. I wasn't really all that hungry, as I had been snacking most of the day on the journey, but they had a lovely array of salad and plenty of choices. I helped myself and then sat down at the table to get to know my new friends. I was well aware of the inquisitive glances of the airwomen as they entered the mess.

Both Barbara and Betty were fascinated that I had been in before.

"Whatever did you come back for? said Barbara. "I can't wait to get out!"

"You will change your mind when you are out," I replied. "It gets in your blood."

"I must admit my Dad always says that," said Betty. "He still misses it and he came out thirty years ago."

"I don't like the idea of the single rooms," I said, as I chewed on some celery. "It must be difficult to get to know the girls all at once."

"It's good if they want peace and quiet to study," interjected a male Corporal who had just joined us at the table.

"Best way to meet the girls, apart from the NAAFI," said Betty, "is to go into the television room in the early evening. Many of them congregate in there."

"I'll do that," I said. "Thanks."

We carried on eating and chatting and by now the mess was heaving with people as they all poured in at the end of the day's lessons in Air Traffic Control or, in the case of permanent staff, had finished their day's work.

Afterwards we strolled back to the Block as some late February snow was falling.

"We'll call for you to go to the NAAFI later," said Barbara, as we arrived back and started to go our separate ways. They went upstairs to their rooms and I turned left along the corridor to mine.

"You are supposed to call it the Junior Ranks Club," smiled Betty.

"Don't worry," I laughed. "I can't get used to it either and our NAAFI at Rheindahlen was changed in 1961."

The corridor was now filling up with sound of voices and all the doors were open. I thought again that it was sad in a way. They were only young and it used to be nice being all together and have the banter between everybody. Now it was through a wall or sticking their heads out of the door and calling down the corridor.

I finished sorting myself out and got into civilian clothes and then went upstairs to where there was another lot of accommodation and the television room. I must say everybody was very friendly.

"Ooh, I bet that is our new Corporal," I heard somebody whisper. "Just saw her in the Mess in uniform."

The TV room was a friendly looking place, quite large and with twenty or so comfy looking leather armchairs and a big television at the end. Already it was on in the background while a dozen or so girls lounged around and nattered. One of them was still in uniform, the whites of a nurse's uniform. She was slim and had fair hair tied back off her face.

"Hello," she said, "my name is Maxime Moss," and then in the next breath she laughed and nodded towards the door. "Watch out for those two Corporal – double trouble there!"

I sat in one of the armchairs and followed her gaze. One of the girls was slim and dark haired and the other tubbier and had ginger hair and a freckled face. Both looked like mischief.

"Don't you take any notice of her Corporal," said the freckled face one, who I learned was called Cathy O'Connor. "We are good girls we are."

The dark haired girl was also a Kathy, Kathy Larley. We were soon joined by another young and pretty girl called Norma Dalzeil, who came from Cornwall. Then there was Anne McCiver, who came from the Isle of Lewes, right up in the Hebrides.

"Well, you are certainly here from all corners of the country," I remarked.

I chatted to them for a while but I could detect certain 'respectfulness' amongst most of them. After all, they had just come from Spitalgate, where a Corporal was 'god'.

It soon became clear though that the two Cathys and Anne were less than amused at the moment. They had been here as Air Traffic Control trainees and had passed all their exams but instead of getting sent to a new and exciting station they had been posted right here to Shawbury.

"Of all things," grunted Cathy O'Connor as she flopped into the chair and kicked her legs over the arm. "How would you like it, Corporal, if you did your training at Spitalgate and then got posted back there?"

I had to confess I would not have been very happy. I imagined being at Hereford on my shorthand and typing course and how my face would have fallen if I had been told I was going nowhere, or much, much worse, Wilmslow or Spitalgate.

"I can sympathise, O'Connor," I said lamely, "who knows, maybe you can get an exchange posting one day?" I knew it was a daft thing to say as soon as I said it.

"Who the devil would want to exchange?" said Kath Larley. She had a point.

"Well, you make the most of your time here anyway," I said. "It all goes too quickly, believe me."

The two girls exchanged glances and giggled.

"Oh we will Corporal!"

I looked at my watch. I was to be meeting Barbara and Betty to go to the Junior Ranks Club.

"I have to go," I said, "but it has been nice meeting you – I am sure we will all get on great."

There were cries of "see you in the NAAFI Corporal!" I walked down the corridor of open doors and Barbara and Betty were waiting at the bottom of the stairs.

The Junior Ranks Club was in full swing when we arrived and the Juke Box was playing the latest records. Whether you want to call it by its new name or the NAAFI, one thing that never changes is the Juke Box. We got ourselves a coke at the bar and found a table.

"We normally go to 'The Elephant and Castle" which is just down the road," said Barbara, but it does get a bit full of the trainees sometimes."

I was happy to sit there and get to know everybody and find out all the gossip.

"Flight Sergeant James seems nice," I said.

"Yes, she is," replied Barbara. "A pity though, because I believe she is leaving at the end of the year. I hope her replacement is just as nice."

The thought of Flight Sergeant Payne shot through my brain for a fleeting minute. No, it was a big air force. That couldn't happen. It had already happened once when she had turned up in Germany after I thought I had seen the last of her at Wilmslow. It couldn't happen again. Besides, she was tucked away at Kinloss as far as I knew.

Eventually the two Cathys came into the NAAFI and sat at another table with some of the airmen.

"Hello Corporal!" they chorused.

Joan Blackburn / Naafi, Nijmegen & the Path to Norway ~ 119

It was a happy evening and I felt sure that I would enjoy my time at RAF Shawbury, no matter how long that time turned out to be.

◆ ◆ ◆

The following morning I rolled out of bed and into the office – well almost. I didn't even bother about going to breakfast. I had the foresight to get myself a packet of cornflakes and some milk from the NAAFI Shop and I had brought a plastic dish with me in my kitbag. There were some advantages to having had the experience.

I heard the key turn in the door of the Admin Office and knew that Flight had arrived. I followed her in and it wasn't long before she gave me a set of keys of my own. Now I had to start work.

"Best you read through that lot," said the Flight Sergeant, "then you can see what is going on, but you had better go and 'arrive' first."

She was right, of course. I still had to 'arrive' and go round the station to places such as the General Office, Sick Quarters and Stores so that I could be introduced to the camp officially and they all knew I was here. It was also a good way of getting to know the station. It wasn't a huge station though – it was just the airfield which had been in existence since 1917 that made it seem larger than it was. Already, as I walked around I could see the aeroplanes coming into land and taking off as the trainee Air Traffic Controllers learned their jobs.

It didn't take long to get the required signatures and hand it into the General Office. At Rheindahlen back in 1961 it had taken a whole day, but here it took no longer than an hour.

I still had the Nijmegen March on the brain as I returned to the office and started to tackle the literature that was still there on my desk. It was February now and the march wasn't until July but the cadets would need to know. I had to ask her and get it over with.

"I hate to ask this, Flight, on my first day," I said, trying to appear as humble as I could, "but can I have a week's leave in July to take my GVC cadets to Nijmegen?" I sat back, waiting for a sarcastic comment, but it didn't come. She clearly was not like Flight Sergeant Payne.

"Of course you can," she said, "in fact I think one of our girls from here is going into the WRAF team and we are doing a sponsored march soon."

Whew, well that was a hurdle out of the way. Now I could let the cadets know and concentrate on my job here in the meantime. It would be my last trip to Nijmegen. I had pushed my luck enough. I turned to study the literature on my desk and among other things there was the history of the station. RAF Shawbury was certainly steeped in the stuff. Apparently the station was here as far back as 1917 when it had been No.29 Flying Training Wing and then in the Second World War such famous aircraft as the Hart, Blenheim, Gladiator and Fury among others flew from here. In 1944 a Lancaster bomber had taken off from Shawbury on the first round the world trip by a British aircraft under the command of Wing Commander D.C. McKinley. It became the Air Traffic Control School in 1950 and in 1951 was honoured by being presented with the Shrewsbury Borough flag at a parade at which 700 airmen and airwomen took part. However, it wasn't until 1963, less than ten years ago, that the Navigational side moved to RAF Manby and Shawbury took on all aspects of Air Traffic Control training as the Central Air Traffic Control School.

"Phew!" I exclaimed as I looked up from my reading matter, "this place certainly has a bit of history attached to it doesn't it Flight!"

"Yes, never judge a sausage by its skin," she replied, "some people think it is a long way from being the 'sharp end' of proceedings but it's had its moments. Mind you," she went on, "I wonder if we could summon up seven hundred for a parade these days."

I left the question unanswered and then left her to go and check out the sheets that had just arrived from the laundry.

The morning and then the day seemed to fly by and by teatime I felt I knew about most things that were going on in and around the WRAF Block. I also learned that we had one airwoman that the Flight Sergeant thought was a bit of a problem. Her name was Eileen Turner.

"Watch out for her," said my mentor, "I have reason to believe that she steals from the other girls. I've had a few that have reported stuff missing from the drying room and also small amounts of money. Can't prove it's her though. Not yet, anyway. Also..." now she dropped her voice to a whisper, "between you and me and these four walls, I think she is queer, or gay as we are supposed to say today."

"*Oh Gawd!*" I thought. Being that way inclined was still an offence in the armed forces even though in civilian life there were many protestors who were bringing the issue to the surface. If you were caught 'at it' you were chucked out and that was that. I remembered there was a bloke at Rheindahlen and once he was found out we never saw him for dust.

"Don't worry," I replied, "I am old fashioned too and 'gay' still means happy and bright to me."

But I had only just come off of the Admin Course and I, more than anybody, knew that things were gradually changing and you had to be so careful when handling such a subject. You had to have real proof and then they were thrown out just as they were ten years ago. However, when the comedian Larry Grayson opened his act on the television with the words "what a gay day!" most people over the age of thirty never grasped the connotations of it and genuinely thought he meant 'bright and happy'.

Oh well, that was a bridge I would have to cross if and when I got to it. It would be down to me as Flight Sergeant James did not live in the Block. I did.

I did see the famous LACW Turner later that evening. She was very tall and very slim with short dark hair closely cropped like a man and no makeup. She seemed to be particularly friendly with the girl in the room opposite to me, but she seemed polite enough. However, it was a mental note made which might be needed in the future.

◆ ◆ ◆

Despite the revelations about Turner, she gave me no trouble so far and the weeks went by fairly uneventfully as I got used to being the WRAF Admin Corporal, a job which was very varied, ranging from simply changing a light bulb to listening to airwomen's problems and, though badly, joining in with some of their gym activities. The PTIs suffered me in silence. I got to know the Cathys quite well though – in more ways than one. They were not bad girls, just mischievous and you could bet if anyone came in late at the end of the night it would be them and they would be drunk. I suppose there were times when I should have put them on a charge but I didn't have the heart. Instead I remembered the instruction I had at RAF Northwood and playacted my rage. Even that usually ended in laughter.

Quite often I would end up down at the 'Elephant and Castle' with them and we would have a happy evening all together with some of the young men from the camp. They were always trying to get me off with someone but all were too young for me.

"Come on Corporal," said Kathy Larley, "look, he'll do for you!" and she would be pointing to some young man who was almost young enough to be my son.

"No, not for me Larley," I replied, "I'll stick to being an old maid."

"Oh come on," O'Connor would join in, "you know you want to Corporal."

"No I don't!" I retorted. So the banter would go on.

I helped Barbara Frazer plan a route for the sponsored march which was to take place the week before Easter. Most of the girls just did it for a laugh and we had to plan it so that we went past the Elephant and Castle and the Fox and Hounds, but nevertheless we did raise a few hundred pounds for local charities. It was a hard slog around a circular route that took us in a southerly direction before going round towards Wem and back down to Shawbury again, but there were very few blisters and most of the girls arrived back wishing they could do the Nijmegen March, though I did have to explain that we did not normally stop in pubs en-route in Holland if we wanted to complete the march and get our medals! Unfortunately, though, it was now so popular that organisations had to register their team months in advance and only one girl from our Station would be able, or could be spared, to take part in the WRAF team. She was a little dark haired airwoman called Jean Ripley, so the sponsored march was good practice for her. Everybody else would have to wait for another year. I was already registered with the cadets.

"I wouldn't mind going to Nijmegen with your girls," said Maxime as we flopped down into the armchairs in the TV room and somebody put the television on. "I could be your cycle orderly – how about that?"

Well, that was out of the blue! True, I had been moaning because the Officer that had taken over from me with the cadets had written to say our cycle orderly had dropped out and I didn't really want to do it again. I had done it last year. However, I didn't expect Max to volunteer.

"Honest, I would do it, if they would have me," she went on, "don't forget, I live down your way – I know where the Brooklands Cadet Unit is."

She was also a nurse, so she would be very handy to have with us.

"I'll tell you what," I replied. "I will check it out with our GVC Headquarters and if they are happy then so am I, that is, if you can get leave OK from the medical centre?"

"Well, God help your backside," laughed Cathy O'Connor, "I'm off to the NAAFI, anybody coming? I need a few beers down me after all that exercise." Cathy always got her priorities right.

By the time we had all had showers and got changed it was well into the evening when we all strolled over the road and into the Junior Ranks Club. It was a beautiful June day and not far off from my birthday when I would be thirty-one. There were, of course, plenty of people around of my age but many more where I was nearly old enough to be their mother. Or at least I felt like it when I went up to the counter for a Coke. There was still 'Chirpy chirpy cheep cheep' on the Juke Box but you couldn't jive to it the same as you could to the Elvis and Tommy Steele records we had in the 60s. But it was all pleasant enough. We were all still trying to get used to the new money though. It was like being in a foreign country when we handed over our cash for our drinks.

"I'll never get used to the idea that a half crown is now 12½ pence," I moaned.

"It's all to do with the Common Market," said one of the blokes in the queue. "We are going to have to get used to it."

"Huh!" I grunted. I still didn't know why they had to change that which was not broken.

I got my drink and went over to the back of the room where there was a long bench seat against the window. The rest of the girls were scattered around nearby arguing about what next to put on the Juke Box.

Suddenly I was aware of a young man arriving and sitting down on the bench seat a few yards up from me. I only saw him out of the corner of my eye because I was busy joining in the conversation with the girls but it was enough to notice that he was not as young as the majority of trainees and airmen. In fact, he looked like he was much the same age as me, which made a change. I was aware of the interest being shown among the airwomen, so much so, that they stopped their giggling and shuffled their chairs over to be nearer to my table. Clearly one

The sponsored march volunteers.
First three from left in the front row: F/S James, Maxime, Cathy.
Me: 7th from the left.

or two of the girls who worked in the Communications Centre knew him.

"I think he comes on detachment every so often," whispered Anne.

He was busy reading the paper so we left him to it and began talking about the sponsored march we had just done and the forthcoming event in Holland.

"Well, I think you are totally mad," said Norma. "I know I wouldn't do it."

Inevitably the conversation led to the Central Band and how brilliant they were.

"I played in a band the last time I was in," I told them.

"No way!" exclaimed Cathy. "You never told us that before!"

Actually, I had been in the Signals Command Band. It was voluntary and for us girls it had been a good skive more than anything. My friends June and Jan had been drummers and I played the trumpet – not very well, but I got by.

That revelation kept the conversation going for a while but all the time I was aware of the young man sitting on the bench seat a few yards away.

He had now folded his paper up and I could sense he was becoming interested in what I was saying. Cathy tried to drag him into the conversation.

"Would *you* do the Nijmegen March?" she asked.

"Not on your life!" he replied in a broad northern accent. He nodded towards the girls from the Commcen. "Anyway, I am only here on detachment for a couple of weeks to help out that lot."

He was quite pleasant looking, clean shaven and with dark hair. Nobody would say he was 'tall, dark and handsome' – he wasn't much taller than me, but I felt quite drawn to him. Not a lot of good though, if he was only here on detachment.

"What's your name?" I asked.

"Norman."

'Oh gawd,' I thought 'whoever calls their child Norman?'

I racked my brains to see if I could think of anyone in films with the name Norman, but all I could think of was Norman Wisdom and Norman Collier.

I didn't even bother telling him my name and he didn't ask, but he stayed on and we were joined by one or two of the men he had got to know in the few days since he came to the station. Nijmegen and the bands were forgotten as the beer continued to flow and I learned a bit more about him. He came from Manchester but he was here on detachment from RAF Valley. He had been in the RAF for twelve years and been to such places as Kenya and Bahrain.

Then, the chat drifted back to the marching again and for some unaccountable reason we suddenly found ourselves comparing feet and shoes.

"Oh, I have got very small feet," said Norman. "I bet I could fit into your shoes!"

I was a size seven.

"Nah, I bet you can't."

"Come on Corporal," said Cathy, "swap and let's find out."

We sat side by side and he put my court shoes on while I put on his lace ups. My shoes were a bit of a tight fit but he could get them on. I could certainly get his on. We both stood up together and with my shoes on he was taller than me. It was a silly thing but it all ended in much mirth.

I managed to retrieve my shoes and started to make a move.

"Anyway, I had better get on back," I said, "work in the morning for all of us."

"I'll walk back with you," said Norman gallantly.

"Oooooh Corporal!" came the cry from the Cathys and Norma.

"Don't get any ideas," I laughed, "he is just being gallant."

I really wasn't bothered whether he walked me back or not, and I was still trying to get used to the name Norman. In any case, he didn't have a lot of choice if he was leaving at the same time as me because his Block was only just up the road from mine.

It was only just starting to get dark when we crossed the road and arrived outside the WRAF Block. We were deep in conversation and carried on with it whilst we just stood in the warm June evening. He was telling me that he was an only child and that his mother was almost blind. We were still there chatting when the two Cathys crossed the road and walked past us up the path to the door. The pair of them were really quite drunk so I got a chorus of "here comes the Bride" sung at me. They thought it was highly funny.

"Anyway, must go" I said, "take no notice of them. By the way, my names Joan..."

"I know," he replied. "I found that out twelve years ago."

"What?" I laughed. "Honest?"

I could see the broad grin on his face in the lamplight. I was totally taken aback and lost for words. "Did you or did you not go to RAF Haydock with the Signals Command Band back in 1960?" He was enjoying himself now.

"Well, yes," I replied, totally puzzled.

In the summer months we travelled all over the country playing at the C-in-C's Inspections. I had learned to play the trumpet, after a fashion, and our Bandmaster, or 'Bandy' as we called him, was so keen to include the girls, that he was quite happy for the brilliant musicians to make up for the deficiencies of one or two! There were only about six girls involved but it was at a time when the Central Band was all male with a separate WRAF Central Band, so we were quite unusual to be mixed. We would have been memorable for that reason.

"I was stationed at Haydock and I remember the band coming into the Mess. A group of us sat with you and I asked you your name."

Now he mentioned it I did have a vague recollection but so much had happened since then, I had forgotten the incident.

"I saw you in the NAAFI the other day," he said, "and I thought I recognised you."

"Crafty bugger" I thought *"so that is why he accidentally on purpose saw the need to sit on the bench near me."*

"Blimey!" I exclaimed, "talk about life being a series of circles – they say that the RAF is getting smaller but this is getting ridiculous."

"It's OK," he laughed, "I just knew that I had seen you with the band at Haydock but I only just remembered your name as we were walking back just now."

"Small world!" I said.

With that I said goodnight to him and he walked off towards his Block. I suppose I should have been flattered that he remembered me after all this time, particularly as it was just a chance encounter in the Mess, Anyway, apart from the surprise that he knew my name, I wasn't all that bothered. After all, he would be going back to Valley in a fortnight and I would probably never see him again.

◆◆◆

Flight Sergeant James was a great NCO to work for. She was kind and hard working and she made my job so very easy. I soon learned that she came from the Isle of Wight and had once visited Parkhurst Prison. She told me every time she went round the Block on a room inspection.

"You know Corporal, the prisoners in Parkhurst have better accommodation than this," she would say.

It was true, the rooms were very small but most of the airwomen made the best out of them and turned them into their own individual spaces.

She gave me an enormous amount of time off for practising for Nijmegen and was genuinely interested in the cadet unit that I had left behind in the hands of another person.

"It must have been a wrench for you," she said, "especially after you had built it up."

"It was Flight," I replied, "but worth it I hope."

"Well I wish I was coming with you to Nijmegen," she said, "but I'll leave it to you younger ones."

"You know that SACW Moss is coming as my cycle orderly don't you Flight?" I reminded her.

"Just signed her leave form," she replied.

If I stopped to think about it for too long, it had been a very hectic year. I had been nearly drowned in a canoe, up a flippin' mountain, met my long lost 'love' from Rheindahlen and some bloke called Norman who remembered me from way back, and now, here I was planning my next and last venture to Holland. Nobody could say it had been boring.

It was 'Freddy and the Dreamers' that caused me to see Norman again. I walked over to the Mess for my tea and all the talk in the queue was of the famous Manchester group appearing live at RAF Tern Hill and that there was a crowd going from Shawbury. I found him standing behind me.

"Do you want to go?" he said "I can give you a lift in my car if you want to."

"Ooh Corporal!" That was Cathy O'Connor!

Actually, I wouldn't have minded going and it was nice to be in the company of someone who had joined the RAF in 1959, as I had done.

"Okay," I heard myself saying.

"I'll see if I can get tickets," he said. "I'll meet you in the NAAFI later."

I carried on along the servery and helped myself to some fish and chips and then went and found a table where the Corporals were sitting and the talk turned to more pressing matters such as who was going to win Wimbledon this year – Billy Jean King or Yvonne Goolagong.

I gave Norman a wave as I left the Mess and went back to the Block. I still had not got my head around his name. Why couldn't he be something more macho like William or Dave? He was a nice enough bloke though and despite myself I found myself looking forward to the trip to Tern Hill.

That evening he informed me that he had got the tickets and the show was on tomorrow night. Needless to say, the Cathys had a field day out of it and there were several choruses of 'Here comes the Bride'. Being the WRAF Admin Corporal did have a price to pay.

"Gosh, it's boring in here tonight," said Kath Larley suddenly, "why don't we all go down the Ellie for a drink?"

There were about a dozen or so younger ones just sitting around but at her words they started to stir. The 'Elephant and Castle' was the local pub and only a few hundred yards off camp and it was a nice evening. From my own point of view I wasn't all that interested. There were some good programmes on television tonight and I would be happy to just go to the television room in the Block.

"Yes, come on, let's go," said Norma, "come on Corporal!"

"No, I'll get back to the Block, but you all have a good time."

"What about you Norman?" asked Cathy O'Connor, "come on, don't be a spoil sport."

"No, I've got to go back to the Block and get some jobs done and I must phone my parents – they don't even know I am here – they still think I am at Valley."

Everyone started to make towards the door and he seemed to have an afterthought.

"I'll tell you what – I may come down to the Ellie later, just for the last half hour."

With that, everyone went their separate ways and I found myself walking as far as the Block with the two Cathys and Norman. He waved goodbye when we reached the 'hallowed ground of the WRAF Block which no man is allowed to pass'.

"I don't want to incur the wrath of WRAF Admin," he grinned.

"Fat chance," I laughed, "I'm WRAF Admin!"

But the Block was also patrolled by MOD Police, so it wasn't just me that kept male visitors at bay.

"Come on Corporal, come down to the Ellie," said Cathy. "You heard him, he is coming down later. Come on, how can we do our matchmaking if you are watching television?"

But I was insistent. Most of them were young and I really did not fancy going down to the Elephant and Castle. I was their Corporal and I didn't want to cramp their style. Besides, Norman had reminded me that I had a phone call to make too, to my parents who I hadn't had a chance to write to in ages.

"He won't come back," I laughed. "I bet he doesn't."

"If he does come back," went on Cathy, "we shall come back and fetch you, won't we Kath?"

"Yes we will!" said Kath. "It's not far, so don't get too comfortable watching television."

I laughed and watched them run up the road to catch up with the others.

I let myself into my room, kicked off my shoes and then walked down the corridor to where the telephone was attached to the wall and phoned my parents. Mum was full of the forthcoming nuptials of my brother, so I didn't have a lot of time to tell her much but at least she knew that she would need to get my youngest brother out of my bedroom for a few days and that she would have another mouth to feed because I was planning to come home for some leave.

I climbed up the stairs to the TV Room and passed Eileen Turner in the corridor. She looked taller and more manly than ever.

"Good evening Turner," I nodded.

"Good evening Corporal," she answered, and went off in the general direction of the washrooms. I didn't like her but there was nothing I could prove. There had been no more reports of money missing and I certainly could not put her on jankers for looking manly.

I switched the television on and settled down to watch The Persuaders. I smiled to myself – that was appropriate considering all the persuading that the two Cathys had just been doing. But Tony Curtis and Roger Moore – that would do for me! If I had told the girls of my chance meeting with Norman twelve years ago at Haydock they would have had a field day out of me. I decided that what they didn't know wouldn't hurt them.

I was just half way into the plot, and enjoying the sight of Tony Curtis, when there came a commotion from the direction of the corridor and the familiar laughter of the two Cathys. By now I had been joined by other airwomen who were all busy drooling at the famous film stars who had been around since we had been children. There were cries of "shh, shh!" but it had no effect.

"Come on Corporal, you are coming with us, he is at the Ellie and we have told him we are coming to fetch you and that is that."

"Oh blimey you two," I sighed, "is there no peace for the wicked. I really wasn't that bothered but in order not to spoil the programme for the rest of the girls I left my comfortable armchair and followed them down the corridor. They had both already had quite a good start on the alcohol.

"Well, give me five minutes" I said, "I have to make myself look beautiful!"

"Five minutes!" insisted Kath Larley. The airwomen were bossing *me* around. I was beginning to wonder who was the boss round here.

I went into my room, brushed my hair and put a bit of lippy on and soon joined them to walk down the road in the summer evening. It was still light and as it was near to mid-summers day it probably would be for some while yet.

The Elephant and Castle was packed and we really had to push our way through to get in the door but there was Norman, sitting with a group of airmen, and I had to admit his face did light up as he realised I was there.

Cathy O'Connor clearly knew the chap in the next seat to Norman and shoved him out of the way.

"Right, out of there Taff," she cried, "make way for the Corporal!"

I felt myself blushing but sat down and Norman struggled through the crowd to the Bar to get me a drink. The two Cathys looked very smug indeed.

It did turn into a lovely evening and after a few drinks he let slip to the assembled company that our paths had crossed all those years ago at Haydock Park. Well, that was fuel to the fire for the Cathys.

"Ooh Corporal, it's an omen," they giggled, and there were more choruses of 'Here comes the Bride.'

"Take no notice," I laughed. "They are both drunk!"

We all marched back up to camp in our groups and parted company at the Blocks. There was more singing from the group that were with us as they all ambled off to bed, and then suddenly we were alone under the stars. We never seemed to run out of conversation and still remained there for ages chatting away. Suddenly there was a kiss and then another and I knew that this man might come to mean more to me than just an acquaintance. Maybe he did not have the tall dark and handsome looks of Richie and maybe he didn't have the attraction of ending up in Acker Bilk's Paramount Jazz Band like Tommy, but I had been young then. Things were different now. However, there was still one big problem. He was only going to be at Shawbury for another week and then he would be going back to his permanent station.

"But I will be coming back here in another couple of weeks for another detachment," he said "and then, if I may, I would like to take you up to Manchester to meet my parents."

My head was reeling.

"Hey slow down a bit," I laughed, "it was just a kiss."

We parted company, but not before we made arrangements to meet the following day for our trip to see Freddy and the Dreamers. It was then that I learned that he had his own car, a blue Ford Cortina and that we would be going to Tern Hill in that.

"I'll park at the back of the WRAF Block," he said, as he gave me another kiss goodbye.

I felt as though I was in a dream. This wasn't happening. After all, I was back in the WRAF for the long haul. OK, it was nice to have some male company, even a boyfriend. I hoped he wasn't expecting too much though. But still, I felt strangely flattered that he should fancy me. The name Norman might be a cross that I would have to bear!

RAF Tern Hill had done Freddy and the Dreamers proud. They had really opened up their doors and the Junior Ranks Club had been transformed into a theatre with the Bar at the back. We all sat at the back leaving the front seats for the permanent staff of the station. The Group were fantastic and sang their hearts out for an hour and a half. A crowd of us found a large round table which was within easy reach of the bar but which gave us a good view of the stage and it was an altogether magical evening. It seemed odd to think that I was actually there on a date.

Freddy pranced around on the stage doing his usual leaping and jumping to "You were made for me" and then the more sedate "I Understand" which was to the tune of Auld Lang Syne. There were also many more songs from other groups such as The Beatles and Buddy Holly and the Crickets. The evening flew by, the drinks flowed and everyone seemed so carefree and happy as we gave him a standing ovation.

Norman, of course, could not drink as he was driving but most people were a little the worse for wear as we all drove back in our various modes of transport. There was even a RAF bus laid on for some people.

Suddenly it was all over and we were back at the Block. We sat in the car and chatted and I wondered how long this would go on for. It was a bit of a no-hoper if he only had a couple of detachments. He even mentioned that he was due to be posted abroad in the Autumn so I wasn't exactly full of hope that this was going to go anywhere. There were a few more kisses and then I left him and went in the back entrance of the Block and came face to face with little Jean Ripley who was doing the Nijmegen March with the WRAF team. I suddenly realised that I would have to focus on the job in hand. True, all the arranging was being done for me, but I had not had much practice and there was Jean to remind me that it was not far off. It was just as well that my trip home to see my parents and my cadets would coincide with Norman going back to RAF Valley.

◆ ◆ ◆

Spring had certainly sprung when I arrived back at Shawbury after Easter and I quickly learned that life had not stood still while I had been away. Tern Hill were not the only camp to have live entertainment but apparently our Junior Ranks Club Committee thought it would be a brilliant idea to have a hypnotist as a change! I heard all about it when I went into the TV room on my arrival back.

"Oh you should have seen him Corporal," piped up one of the new girls, whose name was Margaret, "he was ever so good."

"Yes, he was so good that he hypnotised Cathy O'Connor and she wasn't even taking part!" laughed Maxime.

"What!" I gasped "how did he manage that?"

"Don't know" replied Maxime "one minute she was sitting in the audience next to me and the next minute she had conked out."

"Ha ha!" giggled Babs Frazer, "this is O'Connor we are talking about. Are you sure it wasn't that she was thoroughly pissed."

"Honestly," continued Maxime, "in the end we had to take her into Sick Quarters for the night – it was a bloke called Paul Barkworth."

Just then the object of our conversation came into the room, looking very sheepish.

"Are you sure you are not winding them all up O'Connor," I said.

"No Corporal, one minute I was watching the show and the next minute I felt as though I was on another planet."

"Well that sounds normal to me!" I laughed.

She wasn't very happy at all the jokes at her expense.

"It just goes to show what goes on here the minute my back is turned," I giggled. "He must have been a very good hypnotist to hypnotise somebody in the audience without even realising he was doing it."

"A bit dodgy if you ask me," said Babs Frazer.

If Cathy had been pulling their legs then she certainly never let on and, I certainly could not imagine her actually volunteering to spend the night in Sick Quarters.

Just a few days after the incident with Cathy, Norman arrived on detachment again. I was now actually starting to think of him as a steady boyfriend, even though I had not mentioned him at all whilst at home. It seemed a bit pointless as, even now,

I couldn't see the romance going very far and I was still focussed on doing my exams to reach Sergeant and remain in the WRAF for life.

I was also kept pretty busy both in the WRAF Block and occasionally getting roped in for work for the WRAF Officer in Station Headquarters. Then of course there were always the trainees and new batches arriving and leaving after the finish of their courses. We even had a small detachment of Army girls who I tried to keep together in rooms on the top floor. I enjoyed my job and I did not see it changing for some while. I was also well aware that things would change all round in the Autumn. He was going to be posted from Valley and Flight Sergeant James was due to retire. But they were both bridges that I would cross when I got to them. In the meantime I met Norman most nights in the Junior Ranks Club or we would walk down to the Elephant and Castle together.

"Do you fancy coming home with me to meet my parents?" he said one evening as we strolled back from the pub. He had mentioned it before but I thought he had forgotten about it, so I hesitated before answering.

"Don't worry," he mistook my hesitation. "You will be quite safe. They have three bedrooms and you will have the second one. I'll have the box room." He had certainly worked it out.

"Well, I suppose so," I replied. It must have been a bit disconcerting because I did not appear too enthusiastic. "What about your Mum, though, I thought she was blind?"

"She can see a little bit, but she is not infirm – she will cope. I can drive you up. It's not far to Manchester from here."

I found myself saying yes, although I did feel a slight tinge of guilt. After all, my own parents did not even know he existed yet. We should be visiting them first.

Nevertheless I got myself a 48 hour pass and, much to the amusement of most of the airwomen, who knew where I was going, I packed a weekend case and we left for his home.

"Tra-la-la," chortled Cathy "the Corporal's going on a dirty weekend."

"No the Corporal isn't," I retorted.

"Pull the other leg," cried Babs Frazer, as she passed us in the corridor and heard Cathy's leg pulling. "Besides, O'Connor," she twinkled, "a bit more respect for the Corporal please."

Norman was right, it didn't take long to get up to the outskirts of Manchester where his parents lived. He hadn't lived there permanently since he was eighteen. It was a large old style three bedroom council house on the road opposite the Manchester Ship Canal. He pulled up the little front drive and his parents were already waiting for us at the back door. His mother rushed up to us first and gave him a huge hug and then smiled at me with her unseeing eyes. She looked as though she was looking straight past me. She put on her best posh accent.

"How do you do," she said, "how very nice to meet you." I learned later that she thought everyone that came from south of the Wash was posh. She was about five foot six, the same as me but very slender with dark wavy hair which was a wig. Apparently her hair had never been the same since she lost her eyesight as a child when she had a burst mastoid. Tired of trying to manage what was very fine wispy grey hair, she had opted for a wig and it was now part of her.

Norman's Dad looked a bit like Norman Wisdom but he had a voice like George Formby. He was small of stature but very muscular and had been a weight lifter in his youth and had worked in an Iron Foundry all his life.

"Ee, welcome lass," he said. He turned to his wife, "by gum Elsie, let's put kettle on!"

The house was full of memorabilia from Norman's trips abroad, especially Kenya. There were wooden elephants on the wall and ornamental spears and daggers and even a mini drum that would have been used by African's by putting it between their knees.

Despite her blindness his Mum managed to cook us a lovely dinner and afterwards we all went to their local hostelry which was called The Nag's Head. I was soon to learn that, unlike my Mother and Father who rarely drank, Norman's parents lives revolved around The Nag's Head. It was the sort of pub where the customers got up and 'did a turn' and Elsie Blackburn was no exception. It wasn't long before she was up on the tiny stage, something that she was clearly used to, and giving us a beautiful rendering of Shirley Bassey's 'I who have nothing'. She had a lovely, clear soprano voice.

"She used to sing with Violet Carson in the old days," whispered Norman when she had finished. Violet Carson had started her career playing piano and singing in the Clubs around Manchester and then on the Radio with Wilfrid Pickles in his programme "Have a Go" but now she was better known as Ena Sharples in *Coronation Street*.

She wasn't going to get away with just one song and so she had to do another two or three before she was let back to her beer again. She treated us to some of the old Music Hall songs and was rewarded by enthusiastic applause.

By the time we all got to bed it was midnight but Norman was true to his word. I had my room and he had his and there was definitely no hanky-panky. I fell asleep as soon as my head touched the pillow and I didn't see him again until he brought me a cup of tea in the morning.

They certainly lead very different lives to my parents but it was a lovely weekend and I was almost sorry to be having to say goodbye on the Sunday night and get back to camp again.

When it was time to go they both came out to the gate and stood waving until we were down the road and out of sight, even though I knew that his Mum could not see what she was waving at. As I sat in the car on our drive back I knew that I would have to phone my parents up and tell them about Norman. After all, I could hardly just spring him on them for the weekend. I made a mental note that I would do that after Bull Night the following day.

My mother nearly dropped the phone when I told her I had a boyfriend and that I had met his parents.

"Don't be so shocked Mum," I laughed, "I am not past it yet, you know!"

"I know dear," she replied, "but it is unexpected and we are still getting used to our boys getting off hand."

"Mum!" I gasped "don't read too much into it. He's company, that's all." He was a bit more than that but I needed to get her used to the idea gradually. Both my brothers were still at home although they were very rarely in. Mick's wedding was not far off and Richard's was to be in the New Year. Mum knew I'd had one or two boyfriends in the past but nothing had come of anything and she didn't expect this to be any different. I had a maiden Aunt who was now well into her sixties and they were all convinced that I would be following in her footsteps.

"Well he will have to sleep on the sofa if you bring him home," she said, "and you know I don't like smoking."

Actually, we both smoked a bit, almost everybody did in 1972, except my parents.

"I promise we will smoke outside," I told her.

She grunted. She hated the things.

"Anyway, he is very welcome," she said, "just so long as he doesn't mind the sofa," she repeated.

And so it was that the following weekend we made the journey south and he came to our council house for the weekend.

Fortunately he got on very well with everyone and even my brothers muffled their surprise at me bringing a boyfriend home at last. Norman endured the inspection with good humour. He was always going to be a hit with my father anyway because they could talk about all things RAF and Dad could have his trips down 'memory lane' recalling his years when he had served before and during the War.

All too soon it was over. The next time I would be home it would be leave to take the cadets to do the Nijmegen March.

My parents came out to the gate and waved until our car was out of sight.

◆ ◆ ◆

I still couldn't see this romance going anywhere and I viewed my future as one of life in the WRAF and this was underlined by the next trip to Shawbury by Norman. Between leave and detachment he was almost permanent staff at the moment but this time he came with news. As suspected, he was going to be posted – to Norway.

"Norway!" I exclaimed when he told me. I pictured a land of snow and ice and people walking around in Eskimo outfits.

"Yes, Norway, in September," he replied. "It's AFNORTH, or Allied Forces Northern Europe."

"I know what AFNORTH is," I replied, a bit tetchily.

It seemed that the world and his wife were making sure that I would be in the WRAF until I got my pension. But still September was a long way off. I had the Nijmegen March to think about.

~ CHAPTER X ~

My last Nijmegen

It was a lovely sunny day when we left on the coach once again for Nijmegen. This time there were cadets that I didn't know, but Fay and Penny were there, youngsters who had been with me on every march since we began and, of course Pauline Harris, who had all but taken over from me, although now that the 'powers-that-be' had seen fit to join the GVC with the ATC they were back to having a male officer in charge. Consequently many of the girls had left and it certainly wasn't the large unit that I had started, which is why the team had to consist of girls from other Units. I wondered, once again, why people had to change what is not broken. It was such a shame.

We also had with us the Commandant from one of the Units that we were taking with us this time, but she would not be marching, and then of course, we had the addition of Maxime. She went home on leave from Shawbury and then met us at Brooklands, where we were waiting for her with a bike. Thankfully it was a good bike and, after a few practice circuits she felt comfortable with it.

"I don't envy you," I laughed, "you will have blisters on your bum by the time we have finished." When I had taken a bike and I was glad to get off it and walk.

The journey by coach and ferry was uneventful and it was great to see the familiar buildings as we arrived in Nijmegen. Already it was the centre of all activity and the barrel organs were playing and the bunting was out all over every building that could find a place for it. Of course everywhere was a mass of green and orange flags. The cadets couldn't contain their excitement as they climbed out of the coach and ran up the steps of the school. The Dutch Army Captain was there to point us in the direction of the classroom which would be our home for the next week. All the desks were lined up outside in the corridor leaving room for the rows of bunk beds. Well, rank does have some privileges and so I bagged the bottom one. With all the excitement of the younger girls I was beginning to feel very 'old'.

Then I heard a familiar voice.

"Goodness me, it's ACW Ratcliff with her rings up again – we shall have to stop meeting like this!" Of course it was Flight Sergeant Payne, there again in charge of the WRAF team. My heart suddenly went out to poor Jean Ripley. Jean did not have to come here by coach and ferry. Like the rest of the WRAF team who were in the UK she had been able to fly here, but there her advantage stopped. She had the dreaded Payne as her team leader. I sat up on the side of the bunk.

"Not ACW any more Flight," I informed her, "I'm a Corporal now."

"Oh my word, what is becoming of the air force Ratcliff?" she laughed, "you – a Corporal?" She didn't care that all the cadets were there taking it all in. "Where are you stationed then?"

"RAF Shawbury," I replied.

"Oh, Shawbury!" she said, with a note of distain in her voice. "You can hardly call that the sharp end. Now I am at RAF Kinloss, that's the sharp end."

"Anyone would think she was a bloody pilot," I thought. *"In any case, without the people who are trained at Shawbury, the aeroplanes at Kinloss would bump into one another."*

I smiled sweetly and she wandered off to join the rest of the WRAF team. Above the sound of the different languages of the Danish and the Dutch I could hear her voice yelling out her instructions to the airwomen.

That evening we all went in the coach to the Tattoo. It never failed to amaze and it was wonderful to see the children all dancing into the huge great Arena carrying their armfuls of flowers and all the flags of all the nations taking part. Nothing had changed since that first wonderful time when I had been one of the five girls in the first mixed RAF and WRAF marching team back in 1962. Then it had been us marching around the running track that went around the enormous Olympic sized arena behind the Central Band. By the time the ceremonies were over the area was filled with massed bands from almost every nation taking part, all playing in a cacophony of noise and military music. I'd seen eight of these but I still felt tears pricking at the back of my eyes. One felt so proud to be a part of it.

The following day we were up at a silly hour for a 6 a.m. start. The girls got themselves dressed in their now familiar denim blue skirts and WRAF blouses together with long white socks. Maxime was a symphony in white. Of course she was officially a civilian and was neither WRAF nor GVC for the purposes of this march so she chose to wear a fetching pair of white shorts and a white open necked blouse.

"Have you got some padding on your bum?" I said to her as we walked down the road to the market place where the march started from.

"Don't worry," she laughed, "I'll be OK."

As it happened the WRAF team were starting at much the same time as us so they were already there when we arrived and also the ATC and the RAF teams were arriving from the huge tented camp at Heumensoord. Suddenly I recognised somebody I knew among the WRAF. It was Jean Lawrie. Dear Jean, who had marched with me originally in 1962 and who had turned up at Spitalgate on the Admin Course. Here she was once again in the WRAF team. I waved across to her.

"Hi Jean!" I called. "How are you doing?"

She waved back under the watchful glare of Flight Sergeant Payne. It seemed that the air force was getting smaller and smaller.

GVC (in long socks) Passing the WRAF

A German band was already playing rousing songs and it wasn't long before we were marching over Nijmegen Bridge and out into open countryside. Already the girls were doing their arm exercises as they marched. We found ourselves behind a team of Swiss and in front of the WRAF team. Of course Payne did not like that and soon they were overtaking us.

"Don't worry," I said to Maxime, "we will be overtaking them later, and it's not a race anyway."

We let them go but it wasn't long before we caught up with them again and this time it was us passing them. It went on like this until we reached the first Rest Point. Then we lost them because they had somebody who had already acquired a blister. This had to be seen to and so we were back on the road before them and this time marching behind a team of Canadian soldiers.

Soon we were marching through one of the many little villages on the outskirts of Nijmegen and the little children were coming up and holding our hands. The Dutch people were so friendly towards us.

It wasn't long before the Canadians got a move on and disappeared up the road and we found ourselves behind the Norwegians. I found myself thinking of Norman and his forthcoming trip. It was all very well him saying 'marry him' and I would be able to go to Norway with him. I wasn't sure if I fancied that. Anyway, I took the whole idea with a pinch of salt. I was in the WRAF for the long haul, but I did think this would be my last Nijmegen. Enough was enough.

For the cadets that were with me for the first time, every step was filled with excitement. From the people spraying us with Cologne to the others waving and cheering and offering us cups of water – from the child marching along the road with a toy drum to the Central Band of the Royal Air Force, it was filled with excitement and wonder. For the umpteenth time in my life I wondered why on earth the British did not televise it.

The day soon passed without any mishap and we did the full circle to the north of the town, ending back where we came from by crossing the Nijmegen Bridge. The next day it would be to the east, and then to the south and then the west, forming a giant clover leaf over the four days. The third day, as far as the Canadians were concerned, was the most important one for them because the route took us past Groesbeek War Cemetery, where their comrades that had fallen during the Second World War were buried. The third day for me was the most taxing because it had hills! All this time Maxime faithfully cycled back and forth on her bike, riding on ahead and checking the route and then waiting for us to catch her up. Occasionally, as I suspected, she got off her bike and marched with us, but she was an asset to have as our cycle orderly and she soon became a firm favourite with the cadets.

At the rest points we quite often bumped into the WRAF team either leaving or arriving and gave a wave and a shout to Jean Ripley from Shawbury and Jean Lawrie.

Then came the final day. That wonderful day when it is all over and it culminates in the 'last five miles' or 'via gladiola'.

Here all the countries taking part line up their teams behind one another and they march in behind their respective bands. There were of course the Israelis, the Swiss, Canadians, Americans, British Army, Navy and Air Force.... the list is endless and it takes all day to march through past the stands where the saluting dais was and a representative from each organisation takes the salute. For us, it was the RAF, WRAF, ATC and GVC, the Cranwell cadets, Boy Entrants and everything in between, all lined up behind the Central Band of the Royal Air Force. Our contingent was so long that we also had to have the Laarbruch Pipe Band to bring up the rear. If you happened to be in the middle it was an absolute riot of noise, as everyone disappeared underneath bunches of gladioli that were pushed into our arms by the ever appreciative Dutch.

There was a shout of 'eyes right' from somewhere up the front and so I followed suit shouting 'eyes right' to the cadets as we passed the saluting dais where any number of high ranking officers were seated. The salute was taken, as usual, by the Air Officer Commander-in-Chief of RAF Germany.

Then, before we knew it the march was over. We rounded the corner and marched into the market square where it had been all sectioned off for everyone, and as people arrived so buses were there to take the men away to Heumensoord. Most of my cadets and I lay down on the ground in the dirt and let the world sweep over us. Only Max remained standing, holding onto her bike and rubbing her bottom.

We were immediately descended upon by Pauline Harris and Margaret Hodgkins, the other Unit Commandant, both of whom proceeded to rub down muscles and ply us with water. They had been at the side of the road to cheer us in.

All that remained was to hobble back to the school, get something to eat and then party. One or two needed a bit of treatment for blisters but all in all the cadets were in one piece.

The food in the school hadn't changed much over the years so us older ones went out for a meal in a little café that was not

Max at one of the Rest Points.

in the centre of town. That way we stood a chance of getting served. However, after we had filled our stomachs with omelette and chips we were all in a fit state to join the cadets in the marketplace for the revelry. All was buzzing by the time Maxime, Pauline Margaret and I got there. The centre of things on the last night or 'blister ball' as they called it, were the 'yellow umbrellas' -- the sunshades covering all the tables in the massive outdoor cafe. Already there were some of the men from the Pipe Band entertaining everybody as they lay back in the chairs and enjoyed a well-earned beer.

My Nijmegen was over. Tomorrow it would be back to the real world. I would become a Corporal again and Maxime would become SACW Moss. But for now – we partied.

The following day was a hive of activity as everyone got ready to depart. Of course, for us it was just the females in the school, a matter of a few hundred. However, up at Heumensoord it was a matter of thousands of men having to get themselves organised to get their buses off to all points of the compass. It was chaotic enough here – I shuddered to think what it was like at the men's camp. In later years everyone would be at Heumensoord and there would be no distinction between the sexes but for now I liked it as it was and couldn't imagine it any other way.

The coach turned up for the WRAF teams and I gave Jean Lawrie a hug. It was a bonus seeing her again. She was such a lovely refined lady and I was sure her Sergeant stripes were only just around the corner. I waved to Flight Sergeant Payne. She was off back to the 'sharp end'.

◆ ◆ ◆

By the time I got back to camp Norman had been back to Valley and now had returned to Shawbury on leave.

"He must be keen," whispered Kath, as I arrived in the TV room. "He's never away from here."

Maxime was there, none the worse for wear after her one hundred miles, and more if you count the going back and forth, bike ride. Also Anne and one or two others who had been there since I arrived at Shawbury a few months ago. I already felt as though I had been there years.

"Oh, it's a lost cause," I laughed, "he's off to Norway soon."

"So what!" piped up Kath, "think of it, you could be an RAF wife living in Norway."

"Ha ha, dream on!" I smiled.

However, when I went over to the NAAFI he was there waiting for me and we drove off to 'The Fox and Hounds' for a change of scenery. Neither of us drank very much but the conversation never dragged and the time passed all too quickly. We drove back and parked at the back of the WRAF Block under the suspicious gaze of the MOD Police, who were on duty and shining their torches everywhere. It was as if you were committing a mortal sin to park up and the beams from their torches were like searchlights.

"I'll keep in touch by letter and phone," he said, "and we can get married and you can come and live with me out there."

It all sounded so easy. Half of me was taken up with the romance of it all but the other half was taking it with a pinch of salt. This sort of thing doesn't happen to me.

I saw yet another torchlight approaching so I gave him a goodnight kiss and went indoors. There were still people milling around, among them the two Cathys, who had just come in the front door and who were quite pickled.

"Hello Corporal!" slurred Cathy O'Connor, "have you been with Norman?"

"I think you two had better go and sleep it off," I said.

The one thing about having been in the WRAF before is that we have all 'been there' as they say, and I could remember being in exactly the same state a decade before. Maybe a Corporal who had not been in before, and who would have been just finding her feet, would have charged them for being drunk and disorderly but instead I just shooed them up the stairs. There was a chorus of 'Here comes the Bride' as they fell over each other but they were doing no harm.

"I'll tell you what," I laughed. "I promise you, if I do ever get married and I have a little girl I will call her Cathy after you two."

There was more laughter and they stumbled upstairs to their rooms. I was pretty certain they would have sore heads in the morning.

It was food for thought though. It seemed to be a foregone conclusion that Norman and I would get married and Norway would not be standing in the way of it. I clearly loved him and yet there was nothing official and it still seemed surreal.

Between his detachment and leave Norman managed to spend most of the next month at Shawbury and I saw him most evenings but in the day my mind was on other things such as the day to day routine of the WRAF Block. There was still the little matter of Eileen Turner and everyone's suspicions. I didn't like the girl – she seemed to leer at you when you passed her and she always seemed to turn up where you least expected her to be. Like on the ground floor corridor for example. She didn't live on the ground floor but she was always lurking around. Then, one night, after the airwomen had been checked in and the front door locked I heard voices in the room opposite. I had just been down the corridor to the bathrooms and was on my way back when I clearly heard a voice I thought I recognised. It was, of course, not unusual for airwomen to frequent each other's rooms but it was late and I didn't trust her. That's if it *was* her! I stood with my door ajar for a little while. I couldn't go barging in. I would have to have a good reason and I didn't. In the end I knocked on the door and there was silence. The room belonged to a very young trainee straight from Spitalgate. Then I took the bull by the horns and barged in just in time to see a pair of jeans and manly shoes disappearing through the window. Maybe I had been wrong about recognising the voice. The glimpse I saw looked like the tail end of a bloke to me. ACW Brown gave me a guilty look from beneath her covers.

"Who was that?" I exclaimed. "Have you had a man in your room?"

"Sorry Corporal," she stuttered. "He was only here for a minute – it was my boyfriend."

I was sure it had been Turner but I couldn't prove it. I should, of course, have put Brown on a charge, but I felt it was the man who should be charged and I would do so if I could find out who he was. Then I suddenly realised I was wasting time here.

"OK Brown," I said, "I will see you in the morning, report to me at 8.30 am."

I left her to it and ran upstairs to where Turner's room was. I was just in time to see her coming down the corridor from the washroom in her pyjamas. I couldn't prove a thing and if it had been her I couldn't prove how she got back in. I could only assume she had run round the back of the Block and got in through one of the back windows. She must have moved very swiftly though.

I vowed I would get her one day.

A very embarrassed ACW Brown reported to me in the morning and I read her the riot act. She didn't need to go on a charge. She was only just starting her Course and nothing could be gained by it. I remembered my Admin training at RAF Northwood and put on my best 'battleaxe' voice.

"It won't happen again Corporal, I promise," she quivered.

"If it does, then you are on a charge, that's my promise," I yelled. "Now get off to work."

She ran off down the corridor without a backward glance and all but bumped into Barbara Frazer coming the other way.

"You should have charged her," she said, when I told her what had happened, "give her ten minutes in front of 'Juicy Lucy' and that would sort her out."

'Juicy Lucy' was the nickname for the WRAF Officer, Flight Lieutenant Osborne. She wasn't the first Juicy Lucy I had come across. Practically every station I had been on had their own Juicy Lucy, as if it had just been invented for the first time, a bit like the WRAF songs which we all thought were special to our particular era. No they weren't and neither was a Juicy Lucy.

Barbara was right, of course, but I always felt it was most unfair that it was always the girl that paid the price for the boy entering a room in a drunken stupor.

Besides, I was still convinced it was Turner and I still believed it had been her stealing from her comrades. I wasn't having that but, if nothing else, my Admin Course had taught me that you have to have proof. Maybe I could have got the Police to come and fingerprint the room but even that wouldn't prove anything. There was no law against airwomen being in each other's rooms and it wouldn't necessarily prove that she went out through the window.

◆ ◆ ◆

Norman's last day at Shawbury arrived before I could even think about it and he spent his time going around the station and 'clearing' from the different sections before coming to say goodbye to me.

"I promise I will write," he said, "and I'll be able to phone and I will be home at Christmas."

Just then Christmas seemed a very long way off. So did Norway.

I brushed away a tear as I waved him goodbye until the blue Cortina disappeared out of sight. I walked back into the WRAF Block suddenly feeling very lonely. But I had to pull myself together for now I had to get on with things. After all, I wasn't a silly teenager anymore. I had Eileen Turner to sort out and my brother's wedding was only a week away.

~ CHAPTER XI ~

To Catch a Thief

My brother's wedding took place on 16th September at West End Church, near Woking. It was a sumptuous affair and, of course, it was an opportunity to see every member of our family, some of whom I had not seen for years. I went into Shrewsbury and bought myself a light grey suit and emerald green accessories.

My Dad looked like the cat that got the cream at witnessing his eldest son getting married. It was hard for him to take in that Richard was going to be married shortly as well. His wedding was planned for the following January. I wondered what they would say if I sprang another one on them. Of course, I got the usual questions from the wider family.

"Well, when are we going to see you married?" said my Auntie Rosa. "It's time you found yourself a nice boyfriend." Or, it was "...haven't you found yourself a nice young man yet?" I was used to it – they had been saying it for ten years.

It was a lovely day though and the reception was splendid. My parents seemed to have a permanent grin from ear to ear every time I looked at them.

"How is Norman getting on?" said Mum, as she supped her second cherry brandy, "he's a nice young man."

"Well, he is in Norway now Mum," I informed her and watched as her face fell.

"Don't worry, Norway is not the moon," I laughed. "He will be coming back at Christmas and then..." I winked at her, "well... we shall see."

"Oh goodness me!" exclaimed Mum "not three weddings in six months!"

"You never know," I joked. "Stranger things have happened."

Man had landed on the moon just three years ago and you couldn't get much stranger than that. I wondered whether I would also be doing 'one small step for man and one giant leap for mankind'. The more I thought about it the more possible and real it was becoming.

◆ ◆ ◆

Norman was true to his word. There was a letter waiting for me when I got back to camp and I started to get phone calls from him in the evening. He loved the place and couldn't wait to get me out there.

"I'm living off camp at the moment," he said, "with a couple of the chaps, but there is good accommodation among the British at a place called Avlos. We could rent a place there."

"Steady on," I laughed, as the line crackled away in my ear, "you haven't been there five minutes."

It all sounded lovely though. I had always thought of Norway as being like Iceland or Greenland but Norman said it was beautiful sunshine at the moment and the scenery was breathtaking. Yes, of course they have their snow and ice but the Norwegians are prepared for it.

"It's great," he said, "and you can see the fiords – it's like the North of Scotland."

The Block telephone was at the end of the corridor that the television room was in, so I always made sure I was in there watching TV at a time when I expected him to phone. It soon got so that the girls also were ready for his call and there would be cries of "there he is again" as we heard it ringing down the end of the corridor, and then a cheer when they turned out to be right. They left the door of the TV room closed though and always left us in peace to have our conversation in private.

In the meantime I had the problem of LACW Turner to sort out and this time it was Flight Sergeant James who all but ordered me to do something about it.

"I know that girl is a queer," she said to me one day when we were in the office.

"Flight, you can't say that," I reminded her, "you have to say gay now."

"Who says?" she replied, "to me gay means happy and carefree."

I suddenly had an amusing thought.

"Ha ha," I laughed, "it gives a whole new meaning to when I was in the Fairy Patrol in the Brownies and we used to sing 'we're the fairies bright and gay, helping others every day' doesn't it Flight?"

I took her point though, it was still only 1972 and although there had been many changes since 1959, the military attitude towards gays had certainly not altered. I started to watch Turner like a hawk especially now as she seemed to have formed a very close friendship with a little Army girl who was here on detachment. ACW Brown had passed her exams and been posted from Shawbury. If she were gay it would be the problem of another WRAF Admin.

Turner and her Army friend both had rooms upstairs. If I saw them coming into the Block I always managed to find an excuse to follow them and if they didn't end up where the TV was then they were in each other's rooms. Nothing wrong with that really, most of the other girls spent their lives in each other's rooms but the difference was that they usually left the doors open – these two did not!

In the end it was Corporal Betty Carter who gave me a chance. She came flying into the office as I was typing out the Rosters for Bull Night.

"Turner has that Army girl in her room and they have shut the door!" she panted "come on, there is an empty room next to them – you can hear what is going on."

I walked along behind her and went to go up the stairs as she started for the main door out of the building.

"All yours!" she said, "I have to go to work."

"Oh no you don't," I grabbed her shoulder. "I want you as a witness, this is your idea."

She reluctantly followed me up the stairs. It was not something either of us wanted to do and we still could not charge a girl for having a friend in her room. Not for the first time I wished that the services had not changed from billets, or even four to a room, to single rooms. Ok for NCOs maybe, but for the younger ones and trainees the tiny single rooms were very impractical.

The Block was almost empty as everyone was at work. I knew that both girls worked shifts so clearly they were on their break. There were a few empty rooms along that corridor at the moment and there just happened to be one next door to where the girls had closeted themselves. Betty and I crept inside and both of us put our ears to the wall. I felt awful. It did sound though as if Turner was trying to seduce the little Army girl. We could hear her quite clearly.

"Come on," she was saying, "come and sit on the bed with me."

"That's not a crime," I whispered to Betty. "There is not a lot of room in there to sit anywhere else!"

"Shh!" she hissed.

"Come on," says Turner, "come and sit on the bed, it's cosier here."

There was still nothing to go on. Nothing that could justify us barging into her room with all guns blazing. Even if we had gone in and caught them in their bra and pants there would still not be enough because airwomen saw each other in bras and pants all the time, especially in the days of more than one to a room.

Then one of them must have turned their radio on because their voices were drowned out. We stood there like idiots for about fifteen minutes, although it seemed like fifteen hours, and then the radio went off and there was the sound of them moving around the room. I whispered to Betty.

"You stop in here out of the way and I'll knock on the door," I said.

I was just in time to grab a sheet off the bed to make it look as though I was inspecting bedding and I went out into the corridor. They opened the door just as I was about to knock on it and go in.

"Oh it's you two!" I exclaimed in mock surprise, "what are you doing here during the day?" It was a silly question and it sounded very lame.

"We are not working until later Corporal," said Eileen and the Army girl blushed to the roots of her blonde hair.

"Well why are you both in there with the door shut!" I barked. I wasn't prepared for the reply.

"Why not?" said Turner.

I looked her straight in the eye so that she would not mistake me.

"Just be careful," I said quietly, "now go away."

They both went scuttling off in different directions. This time I was not acting.

This time I had failed but I would get her. I promised myself I would.

A few days later we had a visit in the Admin Office from one of the trainees. She came and stood at my desk under the watchful eye of Flight Sergeant James.

"Corporal, I have had money taken out of my purse."

"Oh lord, how much airwoman?"

She was almost in tears.

"Five pounds" she replied "I know it was there, I haven't made a mistake."

"Where did you leave it?"

"In my handbag, in my room."

We questioned her for a bit longer and then sent her on her way.

Flight Sergeant James leaned back in her chair.

"It looks like it has started again."

I took to patrolling the corridors late at night but a couple of days later another trainee reported money missing from her purse and then another had some coins taken from the top of her locker. I put a big notice on the Board reminding the airwomen to take care of their money and be careful where they leave their purses but we still got another theft reported. We reported it to the Guardroom but they didn't appear that interested as the sums involved were so small. In the end there were about six in a week and we were at our wits end.

"It might be small amounts," said Flight, "but it's a lot to some of these airwomen."

Having a kit inspection wouldn't prove anything. How can you tell if people have more money than they should, or if you find any hidden away how can you prove it is not theirs – it was mostly only coins. We were so sure it was Turner but there didn't seem to be anything we could do to prove it, apart from nagging them over in the Guardroom to get a detective involved.

Flight Sergeant James was at the end of her tether.

"Well Corporal, if we can't prove that girl is queer, I mean gay, then maybe we can get her chucked out for thieving. I will not have thieving in my Block no matter how small the amount and we will catch her." She stood up, did her battledress top up and put her hat on. "Hold the fort, I've had enough and I am going to get the Police on to it by hook or by crook!" With that she stalked across the road towards the Guardroom.

She was gone for ages but eventually came back looking very satisfied with herself.

"I think we have come up with the answer Corporal," she grinned, "but it will be down to you to lay the trap and I also have to wait to get permission from the WRAF Officer."

I sat back, all ears.

"They can get the S.I.B. to treat some money so that if anyone touches it then it will show up on their hands" she said. "We plant it and if it is taken, then we do a full scale kit inspection of everybody. The police have equipment that will spot the fingerprints of the person who has handled the money."

Well it all seemed like a good idea but there was one small problem. "Which room are we going to plant it in?" I said. I suddenly saw another reason why single rooms can be a burden. There was no telling which room she would go in and we couldn't plant a purse in every one. What we needed was to leave it at a central point that she couldn't miss.

Flight Sergeant James looked crestfallen and we both sat and thought. Then I had an idea.

"The telephone!" I cried. "That's it, the telephone. Flight, everyone knows that my boyfriend calls me regularly from Norway and if the TV room door is open I can see the telephone at the bottom of the corridor. Doctor some money and put it in my bag and I can accidently on purpose forget to pick it up after my phone call."

"It's a good idea," she said, "but it could be construed as entrapment. We have to be so careful these days. It's not like 1959 you know! I also have to get it past the WRAF Officer and we would have to keep it strictly to ourselves. No telling anybody."

"By the way," I said, "Why are the police being so helpful all of a sudden?"

"Aaah!" she tapped the side of her nose with her forefinger. "It seems they have had their eye on Turner for some time. The MOD Police have reported seeing a bloke lurking around the WRAF Block and then they realised that the bloke could be one of the airwomen. I mentioned about our suspicions and they are putting two and two together."

"About time!" I retorted.

It took another couple of days to get the S.I.B. involved and to get the money doctored and then a very nice plain clothed policeman handed me a purse containing the cash including a five pound note.

"Whatever you do, don't you open it now," he said. "Just leave your handbag where you said and we will see what happens."

"I don't like doing this," said Flight Sergeant James, "but the worst thing possible is to steal from your comrades and I don't want it in my Block. I don't want her type either."

I wasn't sure if Norman was going to phone or not that night but I also wanted to get rid of the purse when Turner was around. If necessary I would pretend I had a call. I went up to the Television room and settled down along with half a dozen or so other girls to watch the programmes. Sure enough Turner and her little Army friend were there, much too close together for my liking, reading the papers.

Almost on cue the phone rang – it was as if he knew!

"Oh Corporal!" called Anne "there is your boyfriend calling you."

I jumped up and took my handbag with me and ran down the corridor to answer the phone. Sure enough it was Norman, full of his stories of what he had been up to. He had bought himself a second hand Volvo car and he had seen the 'Circle' as they called it, where a few of the British lived along with American Military and Norwegian.

"It's nice," he enthused, "they are all three floors, only they are only two floors at the back because they are built into the side of a hill."

I let him chatter away but I was also aware of my handbag that I had to 'accidently on purpose' leave behind. I put it down against the wall and carried on the conversation.

All too soon though his time was up and we had to say goodbye, but not before he assured me that he had his leave approved for Christmas.

"Now, will you marry me?" he said.

"Oh, okay then!" I heard myself saying.

It must have been the most unromantic acceptance on record and we could say no more because he had run out of time.

I walked back to the TV room in a daze.

"Guess what?" I announced, "he has just asked me to marry him!"

"Wow!" They were all suitably impressed, even Turner, but she must have noticed that I did not have my handbag with me.

"I'm just going to the loo," she said, as all the others gathered round to congratulate me. Then she went out, carefully shutting the door behind her.

My heart was racing. I'd just had a proposal of marriage and now was trapping a thief all in the same half hour. I sat and tried to concentrate on the television with the rest of the girls until Turner got back and then I made my excuses and left.

"Oh silly me," I laughed, "that's what happens when you get a proposal of marriage – your brains go out through the window. I left my handbag by the phone."

With that I said goodnight and went and retrieved my handbag. I waited until I got back to my room and had a look in the bag. I didn't open it but I could see the contents had been disturbed. It would seem the trap had worked. All that remained was for me to go over to the Guardroom and tell them. I spoke to the Duty Policeman.

"Can you tell your S.I.B. friends that I think their trap has worked," I said. Then I noticed a Sergeant lurking in the back of the Guardroom. I recognised him as being a friend of Flight Sergeant James. Obviously I couldn't phone her up from the Block so I spoke to him.

"Can you let Flight Sergeant James know," I said.

I left the bag with the SPs. There was nothing else to be done that night, but if the money had been taken then there would be a spot room inspection the next morning.

The S.I.B. and Flight Sergeant James arrived at the Admin Office bright and early ready for action. Clearly the contents of the purse had been taken and now the task was to find who.

We, of course, knew who the culprit was but we had to go through the motions of going through a few rooms until we got to hers, just for the benefit of those airwomen who were still in the Block or on shift work. In most cases they were either at work or in the classroom but that didn't make any difference. We were assured by the police that if Turner had touched the money then her room would be covered in the stuff that her fingers would have picked up through handling it.

I followed them around as every room was checked in turn with no result, until we got to Turner. The detective shone his special equipment on her locker and over her bed and there were blue fingerprints everywhere and, in her purse, was the treated money.

"I don't know how that got there," she muttered.

"Oh, it must have flown there," said Flight.

Turner looked so uncomfortable that, in any other circumstances, I would have felt sorry for her, but she was such an objectionable person anyway that it was difficult to summon up too much sympathy.

We had got her. All that remained was for Flight Sergeant James to summon her to the Admin Office where she would be charged with thieving.

"What about the other business?" I said to Flight, as we waited for Turner to appear. I still had the vision of her legs disappearing out of the window in the room opposite me.

"It doesn't prove anything unless you catch them in the act," said Flight, "never mind, as long as I get her out of my WRAF Block then I am happy and I am not fussy how."

There was a knock on the door and the airwoman appeared, looking very nervous, which made a change.

I sat at my desk and felt smug as Flight read her the riot act and told her that she would appear before the WRAF Officer later that day. Turner stood rigid to attention, stared straight ahead and then marched out of the room under escort.

"Well, that's a nasty piece of work that the WRAF can do without," said Flight.

I wasn't privy to the subsequent proceedings but, as it turned out, there was not a lot that could be done. Flight Sergeant James would have liked to have seen her kicked out of the WRAF completely but, despite our best efforts, we couldn't prove she was gay and we could also only prove that she had pinched the money that had been planted. As it was entrapment, they were on shaky ground. She got seven days jankers and was then posted from Shawbury. I never saw her again but, as far as we were concerned, the end justified the means. Years later it would not have mattered about her being gay, but in 1959 she would have definitely been out on her ear. Now, in 1972 Flight was just happy to have her out of 'her Block'. Besides she had other things on her mind. She was starting to get a little bit 'demob happy' because she would be retiring at Christmas. I wondered who would take her place.

Accommodation Blocks – RAF Shawbury.

~ CHAPTER XII ~

Norway or Bust

Once the clocks had gone back and we started to get the dark evenings the time went by quite quickly and before we knew it Shrewsbury town was a fairyland of lights.

"Gosh, it gets earlier and earlier each year!" moaned Flight. She was viewing the passing of the time with mixed feelings. She had been in the WRAF since the early fifties and had known nothing else. In one respect she was looking forward to being a civilian again but she knew that it would be difficult to adjust. Nobody knew that better than me. Even now I still missed the newness and the wonder of the first time I was in. The WRAF was starting to change now – just subtly but I noticed the differences. I wondered what it would be like in twenty years' time.

As far as I was concerned I was more interested in the present day and the possibility that I might be swapping my Corporal tapes for a wedding ring. It all felt very odd, especially as my intended was not even here.

He did phone though, regularly, and he seemed to have it all worked out.

"We can get engaged when I come home," he told me.

I thought of my poor Mum and Dad. They had already had the excitement of my brother's wedding and now my other brother was getting married. Admittedly they did not have the big expenses that the Bride's parents had, but it still took some getting used to. I already knew that it would be impractical to have a big wedding with all the trimmings, neither did I want it, but I still hadn't quite worked out how we were going to manage it, especially as Norman will have used up most of his leave by the time we had got through Christmas.

"Don't worry," he said, "it will all work out, I'll come home to Manchester and see my parents and then I will pick you up and take you down to yours if that's OK with your Mum?"

I mumbled a reply and said goodbye before he ran out of time and got cut off.

The two Cathys and Anne were still at Shawbury. Trainees had been and gone but they were still there as permanent staff. I couldn't help thinking that they would have loved a posting to Norway just as a change from here. All three and Maxime were in the television room when I went back and inevitably they all wanted to know the latest gossip and what plans I was making.

"I don't know," said Anne, "first we get a new Senior NCO in WRAF Admin and then we get a new Corporal – I can't keep up with it."

I wondered again who we might get to replace Flight.

◆ ◆ ◆

The autumn gave way to a cold and frosty winter and Flight Sergeant James started to prepare me for a life without her.

"Of course, they will post somebody in to take my place Corporal," she said, as she started to clear out her desk, "but it might not be straight away."

I wasn't very happy at all. I had got used to her. She was a bit of an old fuss pot at times but she was kind and I liked working for her. I wondered who we would get in her place. I wasn't kept wondering for long though. The following day she came into the office with News.

"I have heard it on the grape vine in the Sergeant's Mess that your new Senior NCO is coming from Kinloss," she said.

My heart sank to my boots.

"You are joking Flight!" I gasped.

"Why? Do you know her?"

"Oh yes!" I sank back in my chair and covered my face with my hands in mock despair, except that, in truth, the despair was not very 'mock'.

This woman had haunted me through every step of my service life from Wilmslow to Rheindahlen to the Nijmegen Marches and now, it would seem, here.

"Don't worry," laughed Flight, "she will probably be different now you are a Corporal."

"Ha, ha, you must be joking!" I laughed sarcastically. But there was more news to come.

"I believe she is a Warrant Officer now." Flight Sergeant James was finding it all highly amusing.

"What!" I cried. "Oh well, that's it then, there will be no stopping her."

"She must have had some pretty rapid promotion," said Flight, "I don't think she has been in as long as me." She was laughing now.

"Don't laugh Flight," I moaned, "it's not funny!"

"She hasn't been in all that long," I went on to tell her, "she is not much older than I am, that has to be the most rapid promotion on record."

I thought back to my Dad. He had reached Warrant Officer pretty quick. He had been demobbed from the RAF in the early thirties but recalled in 1939 at the outbreak of war. He had to go back to being an LAC but by 1945 he was a Warrant Officer. Of course, there was rapid promotion in wartime for all sorts of reasons, but she must have had one of the quickest peacetime promotions ever!

"Well, at least you won't have to put up with her for too long," the Flight Sergeant giggled, "not if you are going out on marriage."

That was one consolation. Suddenly the idea of getting that engagement ring and getting married took on a whole new meaning! I would have married Norman anyway but it was certainly 'divine providence' that it coincided with the arrival of Warrant Officer Payne!

In fact, she wasn't due to be posted in until after the festive season, so that was another bonus. I did feel quite sorry for all the trainees and permanent staff who would be left behind. Maybe I was doing her an injustice? Maybe she had mellowed over the years? Pigs might fly.

◆ ◆ ◆

Norman flew into Manchester Airport just before Christmas and phoned me up from his parents' house. The plan was to spend a couple of days with them before hiring a car and then coming down to Shawbury to pick me up and take me home. I rushed into Shrewsbury to get myself an outfit for my younger brother's wedding and also a few presents and then all that remained was to collect my leave pass and wait for him to arrive. I didn't have to wait long. He was exactly where he said he would be and at the time he said he would be. I rushed out of the block and into his arms, and then flew back inside again to say goodbye to Flight Sergeant James. She would not be there when I got back.

"All the very best Flight," I said, "I do hope all goes well for you."

She shook my hand and I actually detected a little glint of a tear in her eye.

"You take care as well Corporal and look after that nice young man of yours."

I waved to some of the girls as they came down the corridor and wished them Happy Christmas and she waved from the door of the office. That was the last I saw of her. I really did hope that she would settle down OK at her home on the Isle of Wight and that she would have a happy life. She was a nice woman and a real lady – unlike her successor.

"Right," I said to Norman as he put my suitcase in the back of the car, "Walton, here we come!"

By the time we arrived home it was quite dark and everywhere was sparkling like fairyland with the lights in the windows of every house we passed. Our house was no exception and my parents had made the place look like Santa's Grotto with lights in the window and a Christmas tree. They made Norman very welcome, as they always did, and were thrilled at the idea of us getting engaged, even though I was sure that Dad was in a bit of a daze. Three children off hand in the space of six months; it left him reeling.

"We are going to buy an engagement ring tomorrow," I informed them.

"When do you think you will be getting married?" said Mum. I could almost read her thoughts because I had the same ones. *"Am I really saying this? Is this really happening?"*

"Hopefully, in April when Norman gets a few more days leave," I replied.

"April, as soon as that?" I saw the panic on Mum's face. Richard was getting married in less than a month and now here I was talking about April.

"Don't worry," I said, "we are looking at the idea of a Registry Office so that we can keep it really cheap and simple."

"But I want to do my daughter proud," chimed in my Dad. "I'm not doing cheap and simple."

They did see that it made sense though. We would only have a few days and it would not be easy to plan a big wedding with him in Norway. Besides, my Dad was a proud man but I knew he did not have money growing on trees. There were a few things though that I was going to insist on, Registry Office or not – I was going to wear white, my Dad was going to give me away and the wedding car would be my Dad's Hillman.

"What! Don't you want a nice Wedding Car?" said my Mum.

"No, I want Dad's Hillman and we can put some ribbons on that.

I had plenty of time to work it all out and that was what I was insisting upon.

We were interrupted by the arrival of my brother Richard and his fiancée Pamela and the conversation turned from my wedding to his wedding, which was only just round the corner.

The following day Norman and I drove into the town and bought my engagement ring, which was three diamonds on a twist.

◆◆◆

We had a wonderful family Christmas and I helped Mum prepare the dinner while Norman and Dad got to know each other better. Richard was having his Christmas Dinner at Pamela's home. Then, afterwards, suitably 'stored' as Norman's Dad would put it, we settled back to watch The Queen's Speech, something that had been a tradition in our family since I was old enough to remember anything.

We still hadn't worked out the complete logistics of how I was going to get married and get to Norway but it dominated most of the conversation, and of course, Mum and Dad wanted to know everything about this country that their daughter was going off to. They were used to me going off all over the place, but Norway? It conjured up an image of ice and snow and Santa Claus.

Suddenly Dad got up and went towards the sideboard and came back with a bottle of sherry.

"Come on Lily," he said, "get the glasses out and let's drink to the happy couple."

"Well," I thought, "If we do as well as Mum and Dad have, then we won't go far wrong."

All too soon our break came to an end and it was time for Norman to drive me back up to Shawbury, before handing the hired car in at Manchester. His old school friend Bill, who he had already earmarked as our best man would take him to the airport. I would be back home in three weeks' time for my brother's wedding but the next time that Norman would be here would be for ours in April, which seemed like ages away.

Meanwhile I had the delights of Warrant Officer Payne to occupy my mind. I wondered if she remembered who her new Corporal was going to be. I bet she didn't!

◆ ◆ ◆

On arrival back at camp I said goodbye to Norman and then went upstairs in the Block to the TV room. After all, I had a brand new engagement ring to flash at everyone. Maxime was in there, in her white nurse's uniform, along with Jean plus Barbara and Betty. All wanted to have a look at the ring and hear all about my forthcoming nuptials. Even as I spoke, I felt as though it was happening to somebody else. Anne came in carrying a cup of coffee she had just made. She always got an extra travelling day on her leave because she came all the way from Stornoway and it could take her two days to get home.

"I guess we are going to see our new WRAF Admin tomorrow," said Barbara.

"Ha ha," I laughed cynically. "You don't know who it is yet, do you?" They were all ears.

"I'm afraid it is a certain Warrant Officer Payne," I told them.

"Never heard of her," said Anne.

"Oh well," I replied, "You are in for a treat.

"Isn't she the one I met at Nijmegen?" asked Maxime. "She was a Flight Sergeant then."

"Clearly she has been promoted," I replied. "There will be no holding her now."

Somebody leaned over and turned the channel over on the television to *Top of the Pops*. I was treated to Acker Bilk and his Paramount Jazz Band and the sight of my old flame from Hereford days playing the bass. Life is a series of circles.

I said cheerio to the girls and went back to my room. I had lots of letters to write, to Lyn who was still at Brampton, to Pat Seymour and June, both of whom were at opposite ends of the country had small children now, and then of course there was

Jan, who was now living in a flat on the outskirts of Manchester. I had a lot to tell them all.

♦♦♦

I made a point of getting into the office early on the Monday morning so I was ready for the front door slamming and the purposeful stride down the corridor. I was more ready than she was! She took one look at me, her jaw dropped and she came out with a very un-Warrant Officer like phrase.

"Bloody hell!"

"Good morning Ma'am," I smiled, as I got up from my seat. Clearly she had forgotten our conversation at Nijmegen when I had told her I was at Shawbury.

"Good lord, did they give you some Corporal stripes in the end?" she said.

I looked in the direction of her sleeve with the brand new Warrant Officer's badge and her spanking new uniform.

"It looks like you haven't done so bad," I said.

"Yes, it has been pretty rapid," she replied. She took off her brand new hat and threw it on to the hat stand 'James Bond' fashion. I was hoping it would miss but it didn't.

I had already done the duty Roster and I had sorted out the mail but she sat down at the desk so recently vacated by Flight Sergeant James and began checking everything over.

"Stick the kettle on Corporal," she commanded.

I had seen this woman through every rank in the WRAF. She had been my Corporal at Wilmslow, my Sergeant and Flight Sergeant at Rheindahlen and Nijmegen, and now Warrant Officer. Well, it wouldn't be for much longer. I put a cup of coffee in front of her and she noticed the shiny ring on my left hand.

"Ooh Corporal," she giggled, "have you found a man who'll have you?"

"Yes," I took great pleasure in replying, "I'll be gone from here in April."

In fact, I would temporarily be gone from here in a couple of weeks' time, on leave.

As it turned out she wasn't too bad to work for. She had mellowed a bit over the years and, whilst she was still very sarcastic, she didn't have to take me for drill or check my kit any more. Those days were long gone. The younger ones knew she had arrived though and she made her presence felt everywhere as she strode around like a little Hitler. Fortunately for everyone, though, she did absent herself from the Block quite a lot because she was involved with the WRAF hockey team and spent a good deal of time at practices or matches. I never did take to hockey either at school or later but, just for once, I did realise that the sport did have some uses if it occupied her and kept her out of the way.

◆ ◆ ◆

I couldn't think why my brother had to have his wedding in the middle of winter but I made the journey down on the train and I bought myself a thick coat and some nice accessories so that I looked the part. I'm sure, for my parents, it was a strange experience to see their youngest leave the family home for good. It seemed that one minute they had three hulking great adults about the place and the next we were all gone.

Pamela and Richard got married in our local Parish Church and, of course the bride looked stunning as did Carol just a few months before. I reflected that my wedding would be very modest compared with my brothers but that was my choice. More than once Dad came up to me and said "it is still not too late to change your mind and have a big wedding if you want."

It would be too complicated. We hadn't even worked out how I was going to get to Norway, although Norman did have a rough date of when he would be home. Based on this I used my leave for Richard's wedding to book a date with the Registry Office. If dates didn't work out I could always cancel it.

"No Dad, just a reception at home and your car. That will do me," I assured him.

It was lovely to see all the family at Richard and Pamela's wedding though and, of course, by now the fact that there was another one due in the spring had filtered through.

For the second time in four months I saw a brother off on honeymoon. It seemed hard to grasp that the next one would be mine and that if all went to plan it would be on 14th April. I wouldn't be out of the air force completely though. After all I would still be an RAF wife.

◆ ◆ ◆

By the time I arrived back at camp it was February and with leave I would be able to finish at Shawbury at the beginning of April. It wasn't long. It was time to apply for discharge on marriage. I felt as though I was doing it all in a dream. Much of the last few months of my romance had been conducted over the phone. It was a measure of my confidence in Norman that I was prepared to fill in the necessary forms without even thinking that anything could go wrong. From the minute that he and I had swapped shoes in the NAAFI it seemed quite clear that we were made for each other.

I'd heard back from all the people I had written to and now I had to write to them again to bring them up to date with what was happening. It went without saying that they were all invited. Within a few days I had replies back. June and Pat had their children now but sent their good wishes. Lyn and Jan were definitely going to come to this wedding. They wouldn't miss it for the world.

'No fear.' wrote Lyn. 'I am not going to miss that. I will be there and you just try and stop me.'

In fact Jan even offered to be chauffeur for Norman's parents. It was brilliant that she was living and working in Manchester not far from them! She had settled down as a civilian when she was demobbed, unlike myself and Lyn who both had to have a second go. I had always kept in touch with her though and saw her a few years ago at New Year and been on holiday with her. It really was a relief that she could do that for us because, with Norman's Mum being blind and his Dad not being a driver, the journey would not be easy for them by public transport. Wild horses would not have kept them away though. There were also others coming from Manchester but all had full cars.

Within a matter of days Norman phoned me up. He had made his plans too. He would hire a car and then after the wedding we would travel up to Newcastle and leave for Norway by Fred Olsen Lines. He had secured a house in 'the Circle' at Avlos and that was where we would start our married life.

All that remained was for me to go and buy a wedding dress suitable for a Registry Office. I was determined that it would be white so I was able to find a short dress and a matching hat and shoes. I had lost a bit of weight so just for a change I got something that fitted me nicely. It was all boxed up and the next person that would see it would be my mother. I would stick to tradition as far as I could.

The time passed quickly, which was just as well now that Payne was my Warrant Officer, and since the disappearance of Eileen Turner to a new station we had no further incidence of stealing or any other monkey business in the Block. She was another WRAF Admin's problem now. I spent my free time between the Junior Ranks Club, the TV Room in the WRAF Block and making wedding arrangements.

"This has to be the most complicated wedding on record," I said to Norman when he next phoned.

"Just think what it would have been like if we had a full scale wedding with all the trimmings," he replied. He was right, of course.

Meanwhile life at RAF Shawbury went on. Trainee Air Traffic Controllers came and went, and people like the two Cathys and Anne tried to stop aeroplanes from bumping into each other or losing their way. I knew I would miss it even though I was never part of the 'sharp end'.

My 'intended' finally flew home a week before the due date having secured the hire of a car which was to be picked up at Gatwick Airport. It was a yellow Ford Cortina Mark 2. I was now officially on leave, and so I travelled down to meet him. There was just time for us to pop in to see my parents and reassure them that they did not dream it all and my Mother's arrangements for the reception at our house were not all in vain. It really was a flying visit and we only stayed for one night. With both my brothers married there was no more sleeping on the sofa. I had my own room back and Norman slept in their room. Even this close to our nuptials there would be no hanky-panky at my parent's house. In the morning Mum gave us a good breakfast to see us on our way and then they both stood and waved us off at the door until we turned the corner and they were out of sight. The next time we would see them would be for the wedding itself, when Norman would be staying overnight with my brother. I felt for them a bit as they had been used to a houseful of life but now they were on their own.

I had to go back to Shawbury whether I wanted to or not. I had to pick up my wedding dress and clear from the camp. We parked the car and went into the Junior Rank's Club together. Immediately we were greeted with cries of "hey, the Corporal is back" and "when is your demob party then? You must have a demob party."

Norman got the drinks in and we all sat in a big circle joining in with the music from the Juke Box. In that respect nothing had changed since over a decade ago when Cliff Richard's 'Living Doll' was Top of the Pops. Now it was 'Slade' with 'Cum on feel the Noize'. Bit different from Cliff but still the same spirit of comradeship in the NAAFI and married or not, I would miss it.

I still couldn't believe it was all happening but we drove down and booked a room at the Elephant and Castle. One thing was for certain. Once I had cleared from the camp I was not coming back in the Block unless to pick up my luggage and say my goodbyes. However, I was still officially a Corporal in the WRAF until the 14th April, when I would sign the register as being married.

♦ ♦ ♦

The demob party at the Elephant and Castle was no different to any other demob party. Everybody got thoroughly pickled and ended up singing and the Cathys were no exception. I reminded them again that if ever I had a baby girl I would name her after them.

"That's nice Corporal," slurred Kathy Larley. "Isn't that nice everybody?"

Most of the girls from the Block were there including Maxime, Anne and Norma and, of course, the place would not have been complete without a vast quantity of boys, some of whom spilled out onto the street as there was not enough room in the Bar.

I remembered my original demob party which had been held in Germany back in 1963, just ten years ago. It seemed like a lifetime away now and Sergeant Payne, as she was then, had been there to say she wasn't having any drunken airwomen in her WRAF Block when I rolled back drunk. There was no way I was going to confront her for a second time after a demob party so we stayed overnight. After all, just one week later I would be married, I would never see the woman again and I did not care any more.

My head felt like someone had kicked it when Norman drove me back to the Block in the morning in the bright yellow car. I went in to the Admin Office and said goodbye to Payne for the last time. She was really quite pleasant and very unlike the little Corporal I had known all those years ago.

"I don't think our paths will cross again," I joked, "not unless you get posted to Norway."

"You never know Corporal, you never know," she grinned, "watch out for me in every corner."

I laughed and shook her hand. With that I was gone and I ran around the block and said goodbye to anybody that happened to be there. Many were at work but the two Cathys were just making their way down the stairs. Both looked very bleary eyed.

"See, we were right," said Cathy O'Connor, "we make good matchmakers we do."

They both plonked their berets on their heads and started towards the door. I would miss them.

"And stay out of trouble," I yelled behind them.

They waved to Norman waiting in the car and soon my luggage was all piled in the boot and I was on my way to my wedding.

Norman called in at home and chatted with my parents for a while. The plan was that he would leave our hired car there and my brother would pick him up and take him to his house for the night. I had to get my hair done and try on my wedding dress for Mum to see. Dad was busy polishing the Hillman within an inch of its life and he had bought some white ribbons to put on it. He was going to be my chauffeur and nobody else. Mick duly came and collected my future husband and his wedding suit with the air of a man who really did not believe that this was happening to his sister. He was also accompanied by Carol, who had made our wedding cake for us. Bit by bit, everything was falling into place.

Meanwhile my dear friend Jan had collected Norman's parents from Manchester and had driven them to a nearby hotel. Also some of his other relatives were there along with Lyn, together with his old school friends Bill and Irene. Bill was to be our best man. They would all meet us at the Registry Office. For my own relatives, my Aunties and Uncles and cousins, it was no distance. All would be there. I also had others coming straight to the house afterwards including my old school friend Margaret and her husband. I did wonder how they were all going to fit into the little three bedroom council house.

The following day I came down the stairs in my wedding dress to the approval of my parents. It was like a Church wedding but without the church. We drove to the Registry Office and on 14th April I stopped being Corporal Ratcliff and, with a stroke of a pen, became Mrs Blackburn.

I kept to my word and insisted on walking into the room where everyone was waiting, along with the Registrar, on my Dad's arm and he solemnly handed me over to Norman, who was standing there with Bill, just as he would have done in a Church. We took our vows and signed the Register and it was all over in no time. All that remained was to pile outside and have the pictures taken and then ride home in the very shiny Hillman.

This time my mother was driven home with one of the guests and Norman and I sat in the back of my Dad's car. It was just an old cream Hillman but to me it was the best Rolls Royce in the land and my Dad was the proudest of men.

People piled into the house for the reception and it was a good job it was a fine day because they were out in the garden, up the stairs, everywhere. In the middle of all this the parents were meeting each other for the first time. Norman's Mum stared at my Mum with her unseeing eyes and tried to be posh whilst my Mum also tried to be posh. In the meantime some of the men were up to no good with our hired car, putting kippers on the tank and trying to dangle tin cans from the bumper. Then it was time for the champagne and a toast from Dad.

"Please raise your glasses everyone," he said, "I want to wish Joan and Norman all the happiness in the world and a safe trip to Norway." Then he looked across at Mum "...and if all my children do as well as we have done then they will not go far wrong."

He had the look of a man who had just had a traumatic six months and getting used to just being on their own again would be a whole new venture.

With the toasts over, Norman, ever aware that it was a hired car and that we would have to hand it in tried, in vain, to stop my brothers and Margaret's husband Geoff from decorating it with the tin cans. In the end he gave it up as a bad job.

"Leave it Norman," I said, "we will sort it out when we are round the corner."

The fact remained, though, that although I had been officially a civilian for a few hours now, Norman was not. I was an RAF wife and we had to get to Norway. It was time to rescue the car and drive to Brighton for a couple of days before the journey up to Newcastle and then the trip across the North Sea, which I was not looking forward to. There were hugs all round, especially for mine and Norman's parents and also my brothers and their new wives. All the Aunts and Uncles and friends gathered around and again I wondered how they all managed to fit in the house. There would be much cleaning up to do afterwards but I knew Mum would not go short of help.

"You take care and good luck to you both," said my Dad as he gave me another hug. "Come back and see us soon."

When we moved towards the car everyone piled out onto the street to see us off. Norman had used up all his leave so goodness only knows when we would see any of them again. There was more than one moist eye in the crowd as the bright yellow car pulled away, accompanied by the sound of the tin cans that had been lovingly tied to the back. I peered through the window and there were my parents standing together with all the relatives around them, together with Jan and Lyn from my first time in the WRAF and my old school friend Margaret.

"Yes," I thought, "if we can do as well as Mum and Dad, we certainly won't go far wrong."

It would be another eighteen months before I would see any of them again.

◆ ◆ ◆

This is where in most books the writer says "...and they went off into the sunset to the land of the Midnight sun..." or words to that effect. In actual fact, after our couple of days in Brighton, we had the long journey all the way up to Newcastle before boarding the ship in the pouring rain. The crossing was less than calm, to say the least, and I spent most of the journey with a brown paper bag clutched in my hand. But it was worth it. By the time we arrived at Avlos the evening sun was shining and you could almost smell the clear Norwegian air. I looked at the three storey building that was to be my home for the next couple of years. As Norman had said, it was wooden and built into the mountain. Similar houses were all around and formed into a circle around a green area with trees in the middle.

"Welcome to Avlos," said Norman.

Now this is where in most books the writer says "...and then he scooped her up in his arms and carried her over the threshold."

No. He didn't want a slipped disc! We walked across the threshold and I found myself in a lovely furnished house heated by a single stove and with triple glazed windows. The ground floor was mostly a utility room, so I went upstairs, where I found the kitchen and living room. The bedrooms were on the floor above that. I soon found a kettle.

"That's a good idea," said Norman, "put kettle on love, I'm parched."

My married life had begun.

My married life had begun but I had not left the air force. Norman's job was in the Communications Centre at Kolsas, the Headquarters for AFNORTH, so he went off in uniform every day and we soon got to know the British and Americans who lived in the 'circle'. The RAF would never go away completely.

About a month after our arrival we arranged to have our marriage blessed by the English Vicar at St Edmund's Anglican Church, Oslo.

One year later our daughter was born in the Riks Hospital in Oslo and I was true to my word and named her Catherine. She was, of course, beautiful. My parents had the trip of a lifetime when they came to Norway for their granddaughter's christening. Although Dad had spent all those years in the RAF he had never been in an aeroplane. Even during the war he had been transported everywhere by ship and, of course, the nearest Mum ever got to overseas was The Isle of Wight. It was such an adventure for them.

Norman collected them from the airport in his Volvo car while I stayed at home with the baby. Now, this is where in most books the writer would say "...and the parents fell into the loving arms of their daughter" No. My mother got out of the car and ran past me without a backward glance and straight up the stairs

St Edmund's Anglican Church, Oslo.

to where Catherine lay sleeping. After eighteen months I might as well not have been there!

"Where's my granddaughter?" she cried. "Where's my granddaughter?" I arrived up the stairs behind her and she had already lifted the baby out of the crib. I think at that moment she was the happiest person in the world. Dad was only just behind her and I felt his arm go round my shoulders. I hugged him and his face was very wet. For the rest of their stay they could barely take their eyes of the child. I had previously sent them some photographs and Mum informed me that Dad always carried them about his person.

"He shows them to anybody in the street," she said, "even complete strangers sometimes."

I could well imagine it. He was proud of me being in the WRAF and he was proud I had married an RAF man, but his first granddaughter topped the lot.

The Christening took place in the same church in which we had our marriage blessed, St Edmund's in Oslo. Our RAF neighbours Alice and Ken acted as Godparents together with another neighbour Anita and yet another neighbour, Sheila, made the white lace christening gown. It was a truly beautiful day.

Mum and Dad stayed with us for a week and we were able to show them around as much as we could of Norway, from the fiords to the famous Telemark dam that played such a significant part in the war, but always Catherine was with us in the back of the car in her crib. We showed them round Oslo, the King's palace and the wonderful Frognor Park with its amazing and sometimes raunchy statues.

"Oh my goodness!" cried Mum when she was faced with a particularly rude one of men showing all their bits. "Oh my goodness!"

We even hired a boat and took them on the fiords but all the time Catherine came too.

The time went by quickly though and soon we were driving them to the airport. This time it would not be so long before we would see them again.

Our tour of Norway came to an end when Norman finally, after thirteen years, got his Corporal tapes and we were posted back to England to RAF Rudloe Manor.

"About flippin' time," he said, when they were finally sewed on by Stores. It had taken him all that time whereas I, as WRAF Admin, had got mine in one year. It seemed very unfair really. It was all down to trade and vacancies. His pay was more than mine though so that made up for it.

Then, three years after the birth of Catherine, our family was completed by the birth of our son David. If the grandparents were happy before, they were ecstatic now. In another eighteen years' time David was to join the RAF too and the circle would be completed. But for Norman, his time in the air force was at an end, though not completely. He simply changed uniforms for that of a Ministry of Defence Policeman – the very people that were so free and easy with shining their torches into cars at Shawbury and elsewhere.

◆ ◆ ◆

Norman and Me in Norway.

Epilogue

The first time I was in the WRAF I was lucky enough to be stationed at the two best stations in the air force – in my opinion, anyway. I never dreamt that one day I would return to both decades later but under such different circumstances.

It was a lovely summer day and the gardens were a picture as Norman and I drove through the familiar iron gates of RAF Medmenham. Well, actually it wasn't RAF Medmenham anymore. It was now the Ministry of Defence Police Training School and we were going to a Passing Out Parade which was taking place on the sports field where once, a lifetime ago, I had crossed to go to the gym for band practice. It seemed totally strange to stand with all the other guests and watch the new Modplods marching in front of us and to look across at the WRAF Block and imagine it full of police instead of young airwomen. I wondered how many of these Modplods would be shining their torches into cars on RAF Stations to stop couples canoodling.

"Ha ha!" laughed Norman, when I voiced my thoughts. "They wouldn't have to worry these days as they are allowed in each other's Blocks anyway. It's all changed now." He actually didn't do any torch shining because he worked at the Headquarters Ministry of Defence Police in London.

On the face of it Medmenham hadn't changed very much. All the old buildings were there – the Mess, the NAAFI, the Blocks but now all used for something different. What had changed was the Monastery, which had been used for Signals Command Headquarters and the Officer's Mess. It had been sold off and was now a hotel called Danesfield House.

We were joined by a couple of the MOD Police who had just been on parade and we walked around the grounds.

"Oh dear," I laughed, "it just seems like five minutes ago that we were running around there looking for the ghost of The Grey Lady."

They gave me strange looks. After all, I was in my fifties now.

"I was young once, you know!" I smiled.

It had been a lovely little station. God's Little Acre they called it, but soon it would be gone in the mists of time. In a few more years the whole of Medmenham would be raised to the ground and replaced by lawns and gardens, and Danesfield House was painted brilliant white and the hotel became very posh indeed. So posh that it became where George Clooney spent some of his honeymoon. It was now way beyond the reach of most of the airwomen who had once worked and played in and around it.

Danesfield House (formerly Headquarters Signals Command Medmenham)– after the airmen and airwomen had left.

188 ~ *Naafi, Nijmegen & the Path to Norway / Joan Blackburn*

Lyn and I stood and gazed at the three empty and derelict WRAF Blocks. If Medmenham had been one of the smallest stations in the Air Force, then Rheindahlen in Germany was the complete opposite. It was the biggest.

"Oh Ratty, don't they look sad!" said Lyn, as she walked up to the window and tried to peer inside. I had visions of Flight Sergeant Payne coming out to ask her what she was nosing at.

Norman and our twenty-three year old daughter Catherine stood on the path and watched us in silence as we had our little trip down Memory Lane. She was right, they were a sad sight and I could feel the tears of nostalgia welling up in my eyes. The WRAF Blocks stood like empty shells with the grass growing up unkempt around them.

We were visiting Rheindahlen because our son David was stationed at RAF Bruggen and he arranged for the three of us to stay at the Families Hostel, which was located here. The idea was to 'kill two birds with one stone' and visit him whilst, at the same time, taking advantage of the hostel to have a look at our old haunts on this, the biggest non-operational station in the world. It had also been, for Lyn and I, the best. When we left here in 1963 there had been many tears.

"Come on Mum," said Catherine, getting impatient, "we will be meeting David again soon."

It was true, we would be meeting David again to say goodbye until the next time he could come home on leave. Now I knew what my Mum used to feel like.

We pulled ourselves away from the desolate looking buildings. Clearly the airwomen were living elsewhere on the camp, probably in single rooms now. We had been four to a room and Lyn and I had shared the same one at the top of the stairs. Now they were empty and just shells without the happy squealing and singing of the young women that once ran through their corridors. We walked around to the back of the Block to where the washing room windows were. Windows where many an

The Big House, Rheindahlen
(after the flags had come down forever).

airwoman had climbed through in a bid to outwit WRAF Admin who were there to make sure they were in on time. We peered through but there was nothing to see.

"Oh, if only those walls could talk," I said to Lyn as we walked round to the front again.

The four of us walked down the path and round towards the parade ground. Much of the rest of the camp seemed to have been unchanged, except for a few differences here and there. We went past the men's billets, which still seemed to be in use.

"That's where John and Richie used to live," said Lyn.

"Who are they?" piped up Catherine.

"Oh, just old boyfriends," I laughed, "just old boyfriends."

"Gawd look!" said Lyn, "cars on the parade ground – that would never have happened in our day."

It certainly wouldn't. The Station Warrant Officer would have had their giblets first.

Of course we were not allowed in the Junior Ranks Club but we walked past it and could see it had not altered much and the Astra Cinema opposite was still there, as was the YWCA.

"Well, most of it looks much the same," I said to Lyn. "It just seems to be that the trees are bigger – that is what I notice the most."

"Well of course the trees are bigger!" laughed Norman, "you don't expect them to stop growing just because you two left do you?"

It all looked very overgrown and not as pristine new as it had all those years ago. It looked tired somehow and there didn't seem to be so many personnel buzzing about. Of course, most people were at work, but back in 1963 it didn't matter what time of day it was. The place always buzzed with activity and was full of life and vitality.

We walked to where we had left the car and Norman drove slowly around the camp one more time and up to the Big House where Lyn and I had worked. Yes, it was still there and just as glorious with the row of flags of all the nations outside. I felt very proud to have worked there and, even now, I still marvelled at the size of the place. There were a few people in uniform coming and going and an officious looking Army policeman on the gate so we didn't stop.

We had been staying here for two days so we had seen all over the camp and had spent precious time with David. However, we could not leave without just one more drive past the empty WRAF Blocks where we had so much fun all those decades ago. How were we to know that in fifteen years' time the whole place would be abandoned as the military pulled out and everything was handed back to the Germans. In some ways it looked as though they were starting already.

We picked up our luggage from the Hostel and drove to Bruggen, where David met us at the camp gates. He had just finished his day's work as an aircraft technician and was still in uniform. I was so proud and, for the umpteenth time since he joined up I wished that my parents were still around to see him. Sadly my Dad died too soon, so never did see him in uniform. Mum, on the other hand, did see his Passing Out Parade and died a year afterwards. Norman's parents also died within the same few years.

Sadly, it had been inclement weather and the parade had been held in the hangar so there was no flypast, but it didn't take away the pride we all felt as they all marched in to the strains of the Royal Air Force March Past. The tears of pride and emotion had just flown unchecked down my face as I looked at my son standing so smartly to attention – his Granddad was surely looking down. I felt that same pride now as we laughed and exchanged pleasantries with his friends who were standing around with him.

"Don't worry Mrs Blackburn, we will look after him," laughed his mate, jokingly.

David blushed and gave us a hug.

"You take care, all of you," I said, as we left to get into the car.

It was like history repeating itself.

I realised that you could take the girl out of the air force but you could not take the air force out of the girl. I would always have air force blue blood. It was in me, from my Dad when he served in WW2 in France and Malta and helped make Britain a safer place for me to grow up in and also join the Air Force myself, to my husband and my son. As David waved us off and I sat in the front of the car with Norman driving and Lyn and Catherine in the back I felt I could hear the strains of the RAF March going round in my head. Would I ever forget the thrill of mine and David's passing out parades or the excitement of marching in Nijmegen to the sound of the Central Band of the Royal Air Force? I would have to be dead first!

But there was one equal thrill which, of course, was the thrill of the birth of my baby daughter, who was now a bright young woman sitting in the back of the car with Lyn. They symbolised both my times in the WRAF. Lyn reminded me of that first magical time – when everything was new and bright and Elvis was King and the world was our oyster. Catherine was the result of the second time – when things were already changing and we had moved from the simplicity of the fifties and sixties to the more worldly wise seventies. However, without the second time I never would have met Norman and my two children would never have been born.

Would I do it all again? In a heartbeat. But if anybody had told me back in 1963 when I left Rheindahlen for the first time that I would re-join and have a son follow in my footsteps and a daughter called after two mischievous airwomen from the WRAF Block in Shawbury, I would have said, to quote Pat Seymour, that they were 'stark raving bloody bonkers.' Moreover, if anyone had told me when we visited Rheindahlen for the last time that by 2013 it would be closed and that RAF Medmenham (God's Little Acre) would not exist, well... I would have been lost for words.

They are gone now, in the mists of time. However, I'm willing to bet that if anyone who was ever stationed at either of those two establishments were to go to the place where they once were, and screw their eyes up tight and concentrate hard, they will surely hear the sounds of the laughter, the tears when a romance went wrong and the beat of the drum, and if they pricked their finger they might just detect a little drop of air force blue blood.

The End

About the Author

Joan Blackburn was born in Woking in 1941. Her first book 'Naafi, Knickers & Nijmegen' was published in 2009 and told of her adventures in the WRAF between 1959 and 1963.

After the success of this tale of Air Force life in the swinging sixties, Joan was encouraged to go back a generation for her second book 'Granddad's Rainbow'. This told of life on the home front both during and immediately after the war and featured her parents, Lily and Stan. It is against the, fast disappearing, upstairs/ downstairs life of her grandparents where they worked for the gentry and also against the background of Stan's life in the RAF serving in France and Malta and the steadfastness of Lily as she waited for him to come home.

In 'The Tailor's Daughter' Joan went back still further to the Victorian life of her Great Grandmother on Lily's side of the family, who, in the 1880s set sail for New Zealand on her own. Lily's maiden name was Gosley. Her grandfather married the plucky Charlotte Adshead and the decision they were forced to make, soon after their marriage, affected every generation thereafter. This trilogy of books cover 150 years of family history.

Joan is married to Norman Blackburn and lives in West Sussex. She has two children, Catherine and David, and four small grandchildren, Jacob, Alice, Harvey and Keira.

◆ ◆ ◆